RETHINKING INN(

Innovation is the central pillar for corporate growth for the 21st century. Yet while every business executive touts innovation as a top priority, no comprehensive survey has investigated what corporate leaders are actually thinking and doing about it – until now.

Rethinking Innovation: Insights from the World's Leading CEOs is the definitive volume on the subject, drawing its power from the remarkable depth of its background research. For it builds upon the most comprehensive fact-finding mission on corporate innovation in history, IBM's Global CEO Study. That survey involved in-depth interviews with 765 CEOs, business executives and public sector leaders from 20 industries and 11 geographic regions, from mature markets as well as from China, India, Eastern Europe and Latin America.

Conceived and edited by *Fast Thinking*, the world's foremost innovation magazine, this book transforms an immense body of knowledge into usable form, and provides an indispensable guide for the managers and leaders who must drive innovation in their organizations.

The essays in *Rethinking Innovation* neatly summarise the theory and practice behind the key findings of IBM's study: business model innovation matters; collaboration is indispensable; and innovation requires leadership from the top. And they investigate the experiences of many leading corporate innovators, including Google, Airbus, Eli Lilly, Caterpillar, the Korean steel maker POSCO, ResMed, Cochlear, and Nintendo.

Rethinking Innovation delivers a rich view of how leaders are driving innovation, sheds light on which kind of innovation matters the most, and demonstrates the crucial roles of collaboration, partnering and technology integration. This is a publication no thinking manager can afford to be without.

"An important shift is occurring in the way we think about innovation ... and that requires a quantum shift in the nature of the company."

Richard Florida, author of The Rise of the Creative Class

RETHINKING INNOVATION

Insights from the World's Leading CEOs

Marc Chapman, Saul Berman & Amy Blitz
Foreword by Michael Tushman

RETHINKING INNOVATION

Published by
Fast Thinking Books
A division of ETN-COM

J.M.F. Keeney: Editor-in-Chief

Ashley Russell: Group Publishing Director

P+61 2 9418 7100
F +61 2 9428 2607
Level 3, 448 Pacific Hwy
Artarmon NSW 2064
www.etncom.com
www.fastthinking.com.au

First published January 2008
1st ed.
ISBN 978-0-9775866-4-6
Copyright © Marc Chapman, Saul Berman & Amy Blitz
All Rights Reserved.

All feedback and inquiries are welcomed at info@etncom.com

Designed by Nick Dale.
Edited by Hugh Lamberton.
Printed and bound by SNP Security Printing Pte Ltd.

The paper used in the production of this book is from a sustainable forest.

RETHINKING INNOVATION

Insights from the World's Leading CEOs

Marc Chapman, Saul Berman & Amy Blitz
Foreword by Michael Tushman

FAST TH!NKING

"It doesn't matter who you ask, whether it's Jeffrey Immelt at General Electric or Ed Zander at Motorola, we all know that when you have the cost structures we have in the developed world, if you don't innovate, you're dead."

Peter Farrell, founder and CEO of ResMed

Contents

Foreword

Michael Tushman

IBM's most recent Global CEO Study found that most business leaders expect their organizations to face change on a massive scale in the near future. This is a significant finding and one that leads to the question: how do organizations survive in the face of such change?

Underlying this question is a rich debate about whether organizations can adapt – and if so, then how. One, rather grim, perspective suggests that most organizations are largely inert and will ultimately fail. A second, more hopeful, perspective argues that some firms do learn and adapt to shifting environmental contexts. What sets these firms apart from those that fail to adapt? Recently, the thinking on corporate adaptation has coalesced around two themes. One, based on research in strategy, suggests that dynamic capabilities – the ability of a firm to reconfigure assets and existing capabilities – explain long-term competitive advantage. The other, based on organizational design, argues that ambidexterity – the ability of a firm to simultaneously explore and exploit – enables a firm to adapt over time.

In our research on the topic, Charles O'Reilly and I argue that ambidexterity is an important root of dynamic capabilities.

What do we mean by this? In brief, ambidextrous organizational designs are those that sustain current success while simultaneously building new products, services, or processes. Ambidextrous organizational designs are composed of an interrelated set of competencies, cultures, incentives, and senior team roles. These designs are significantly more effective for serving innovation, and therefore adaptation and long-term survival, than functional, cross-functional, spinout or other designs. We have found, moreover, that ambidextrous organizations improve their innovation outcomes in a variety of ways, from exploiting and improving the performance of existing products to cultivating more exploratory areas. We have also found that ambidextrous designs are important for driving innovation *within* business units as well as *across* business units.

Finally, we have learned that one key to the success of the ambidextrous organization is executive leadership. To keep the left and right hands working together, strong senior leadership is needed to resolve strategic contradictions, to establish processes that support ambidextrous approaches, and, overall, to build dynamic capabilities that allow for continuing adaptation.

At the heart of all this is a willingness to find opportunity within change. This requires an ability to innovate, and not just in products and services as is too often the focus, but in the very design, direction and overall strategy of the organization. In the papers that follow, the IBM Strategy & Change leadership team provides a roadmap for innovation, for change and adaptation, for building on existing strengths while identifying new areas of opportunity at the level of underlying business models, as well as organizational design, operations, and technology strategy.

Michael Tushman

Paul R. Lawrence MBA Class of 1942 Professor of Business Administration, Harvard Business School.

Rethinking innovation

An introduction

Marc Chapman, Saul Berman
and Amy Blitz

Over the past few years, the Strategy and Change leadership
team within IBM's Global Business Services has explored a
diverse range of issues related to innovation, focusing on areas
with the greatest potential to lift an organization's overall
performance to new heights. Scaling the innovation summit,
however, is not easy, particularly in today's increasingly complex
business environment. So we offer this collection of essays as
a guide, drawing on the experience and insights of successful
innovators across many industries and regions.

The book begins with the findings from a major IBM research effort,
Expanding the Innovation Horizon, involving in-depth conversations
with 765 CEOs, business executives, and public sector leaders.[1] Based
on the findings of these conversations, we delved deeper into areas
where the promise of innovation seemed most compelling.

Our series of follow-on papers examine innovations in:
- underlying business models (chapter 3, *Paths to success: Three ways to innovate your business model)*;
- organizational strategies to enable greater collaboration among employees as well as suppliers, customers, business partners and others – what we call here the extended enterprise (chapter 4, *The power of many: ABCs of collaborative innovation)*;
- operational approaches that balance efficiency with effectiveness while driving continuous innovation throughout an extended enterprise (chapter 5, *The Lean Six Sigma way: Driving operational innovation)*;
- the technologies that will be key to making all of this possible (chapter 6, *The new rules of value 2.0: How to capitalize on emerging technologies)*.

This book brings together our findings in a comprehensive view of how best to innovate in today's fast-changing business environment.

But first, why rethink innovation? The short answer: to stay ahead of the curve and to grow. We knew, from an earlier 2004 study, that CEOs were relying on innovation to drive profitable growth. But beyond innovation's bottom-line importance, we believed that business and public sector leaders were acutely aware of the phenomenal challenges society faces in the coming decades – and our mutual dependence on innovation to address these issues. In fact, in *Expanding the Innovation Horizon*, two-thirds of the CEOs we interviewed told us they expect their organizations to be inundated with change over the next two years.

Some writers and analysts, like Thomas Friedman, view the world as increasingly flat; others, like Richard Florida, assert that it's spiky; but virtually everyone agrees that the topography is changing in fundamental ways.[2] The forces overturning the status quo are many and varied. At the top of their list, CEOs mentioned market forces such as intensified competition, escalating customer expectations and unexpected market shifts. But there were others. CEOs told us that workforce issues, technological advances, regulatory concerns and globalization are all bearing down on their organizations, forcing significant change.

And their feelings are justified. Think about how the world is changing. In China and India combined, half a million engineers and scientists graduate each year, compared with about 134,000 in the

United States. China is now home to more than 100 car manufacturers.[3] In 2005, the combined GDP of emerging economies increased by $US1.6 trillion – which represents $US200 billion more growth than the developed world combined. And it is not all about China and India – together, they accounted for only 20 per cent of emerging market growth.[4] Emerging economies now control two-thirds of the world's foreign exchange reserves and consume 47 per cent of the world's oil.[5]

Added to these economic upheavals are major demographic shifts. Between 2000 and 2050, the percentage of the world population aged 60 years or older is expected to double, to over 20 per cent. That trend is even more pronounced in Europe and North America, where the 60-plus age group will account for about 35 per cent and 27 per cent respectively.[6] In Japan, 17 of every 100 people are *already* older than 65, and by 2020, the ratio is expected to be closer to 30 per cent.[7]

At the same time, the use of technology continues to intensify. Globally, the world now has more than 1 billion Internet users.[8] Some 215 million of those are broadband subscribers – up from fewer than 5 million in 1999.[9]

Surrounded by change on so many fronts, CEOs do not seem intimidated, or content simply to cope. Instead, they are embracing change. CEOs see it as both reason and license to expand their innovation horizon – to pursue less traditional forms of innovation, to look high and low, outside and in, for innovative ideas and to accept greater personal responsibility for fostering innovation within and beyond their organizations. And they see opportunity – opportunity to be seized through innovation.

Themes from these conversations shaped our thinking, and our subsequent research. Overall, we learned:

- *Business model innovation matters.* Competitive pressures have pushed business model innovation much higher than expected on CEOs' priority lists. But its importance does not negate the need to focus on products, services and markets, as well as on operational innovation.
- *External collaboration is indispensable.* CEOs stressed the overwhelming importance of collaborative innovation – particularly beyond company walls. Business partners and customers were cited as top sources of innovative ideas, while research and development (R&D) fell much lower on the list. However, CEOs also admitted that their organizations are not collaborating nearly enough.

- *Innovation requires orchestration from the top.* CEOs acknowledged that they have primary responsibility for fostering innovation. But to effectively orchestrate it, CEOs need to create a more team-based environment, reward individual innovators and better integrate business and technology.

We also found a persistent, worldwide, sector- and size-spanning push toward a more expansive view of innovation – a greater mix of innovation types, more external involvement and extensive demands on CEOs to bring it all to fruition. Based on these CEOs' collective insights, we offer several considerations that can help organizations sharpen their own innovation agendas:

- *Think broadly, act personally and manage the innovation mix.*
- *Make your business model deeply different* – Find ways to substantially change how you add value in your industry, or in another.
- *Ignite innovation through business and technology integration* – Use technology as a catalyst by combining it with business and market insights.
- *Defy collaboration limits* – Collaborate on a massive, geography-defying scale to open a world of possibilities.
- *Force an outside look ... every time* – Push the organization to work with outsiders more, first making it systematic and, then, part of your culture.

Before beginning the innovation journey mapped out in the pages that follow, we would like to thank all of the public and private sector leaders who generously shared their insights with us. By contributing their ideas and perspectives, each has played an integral, collaborative role in producing the *Expanding the Innovation Horizon* and the follow-on papers. For that we are extremely indebted. And so we offer the insights from our research in the spirit of collaborative innovation.

About the editors

Marc Chapman leads IBM's Global Strategy and Change consulting practice and has led engagements for many Fortune 500 manufacturing and service companies in diverse sectors. He advises clients on issues of transformation, business growth, portfolio development, merger integration, and services strategies. He advises IBM business units on strategic growth issues and his ideas have created several rapidly growing businesses inside the IBM portfolio. He also led the IBM CEO Study on Innovation. *He can be reached at marcchap@us.ibm.com.*

Saul Berman *is the Global Lead Strategy Partner for the Media and Entertainment Practice as well as a Global Strategy and Change Services Leader at IBM Global Business Services. He has worked extensively on issues of competitive positioning, differentiation, new business plans and strategies, new business models, growth, operational and cost improvement, operations/manufacturing strategy, organizational design and enterprise transformation. His clients have included most of the major media companies as well as Internet, telecommunications, consumer goods, retail, and automotive companies in the US, Japan, Europe and Australia. He can be reached at saul.berman@us.ibm.com.*

Amy Blitz *is the Strategy and Change Lead for IBM's Institute for Business Value. She was a core team member of* IBM's CEO Study on Innovation, *and she has since led the research on the follow-on papers included here, spanning innovations in business models, organizational change, operations and technology. Before joining IBM, she led major research initiatives on issues related to entrepreneurship, innovation, and strategy. She has worked with the founders and CEOs of leading companies worldwide. She can be reached at ablitz@us.ibm.com.*

References

1   For readability, we refer to this collective group as "CEOs" throughout this book.

2   Friedman, Thomas L. *The World Is Flat: A Brief History of the Twenty-first Century.* United States: Farrar, Straus and Giroux, 2005; Florida, Richard. "The World Is Spiky." *The Atlantic Monthly.* October 2005.

3   Engardio, Pete. "China and India – The Challenge: A New World Economy." *BusinessWeek.* August 22, 2005; Newman, Richard J. "Motorcars for the masses." *U.S. News & World Report.* June 21, 2004. http://www.usnews.com/usnews/biztech/articles/040621/21china.htm.

4   "Climbing back: The economies of what used to be called the 'third world' are regaining their ancient pre-eminence." *The Economist.* January 21, 2006.

5   Ibid.

6   "A Demographic Revolution." United Nations Program on Aging. http://www.un.org/esa/socdev/ageing/agewpop1.htm

7   Engardio, Pete and Carol Matlack. "Global Aging." *BusinessWeek.* January 31, 2005. http://www.businessweek.com/magazine/content/05_05/b3918011.htm

8   "Worldwide Internet Users Top 1 Billion in 2005." Computer Industry Almanac press release. January 4, 2006. http://www.c-i-a.com/pr0106.htm

9   "USA Leads Broadband Subscriber Top 15 Ranking.Worldwide Broadband Subscribers Will Top 215M in 2005." Computer Industry Almanac press release. November 14, 2005. http://www.c-i-a.com/pr1105.htm

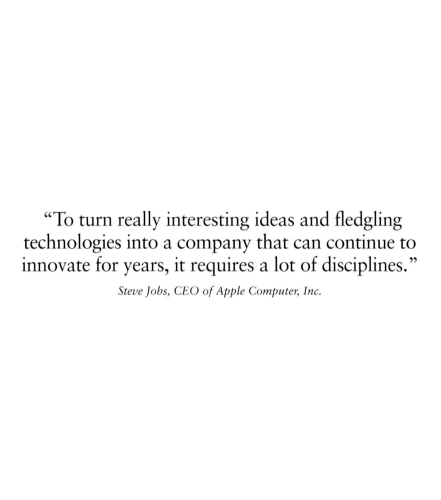

"To turn really interesting ideas and fledgling technologies into a company that can continue to innovate for years, it requires a lot of disciplines."

Steve Jobs, CEO of Apple Computer, Inc.

"Speaking Out: Apple's and Pixar's Steve Jobs." BusinessWeek Online. August 25, 2003.
http://www.businessweek.com/magazine/content/03_34/b3846633.htm

Expanding the innovation horizon

Insights from the world's leading CEOs

In order to find out what CEOs are thinking about innovation, the IBM CEO Study team conducted in-depth interviews with 765 CEOs, senior executives and public sector leaders from around the world. Their organizations spanned 20 industries and included companies large and small, public and private. We also measured how innovation choices affected financial performance. Three key themes emerged: business model innovation matters; external collaboration is indispensable; and innovation requires orchestration from the top.

The overall intent of this major research program was to capture CEOs' current views on innovation. We wanted to learn what was on their innovation agendas, where their innovative energies were focused, and what they were doing to enable innovation. For the purposes of our discussions, we defined innovation as: using new ideas or applying current thinking in fundamentally different ways to effect significant change.

We also widened the aperture on innovation, focusing on three broad types:

- Business model innovation, in the structure and/or financial model of the business;
- Operational innovation that improves the effectiveness and efficiency of core processes and functions;
- Products/services/markets innovation applied to products or services or "go-to-market" activities.

The findings in this paper are based on in-depth, consultative interviews with 765 CEOs, business executives and public sector leaders from around the world, spanning 20 industries and 11 geographic regions (including representation from mature markets and from important developing markets such as China, India, Eastern Europe and Latin America – see Figure 1). Our sample comprised leaders of companies both large and small, some public and some privately held. The interview format and the substantial sample size provided tremendous opportunities for both qualitative and quantitative analysis.

In addition to analyzing the survey responses, we wanted to ascertain whether the choices CEOs were making about particular types of innovation and key enablers had any correlation with financial performance. So we looked at a subset of our sample

Figure 1. **Number of responses by region.**

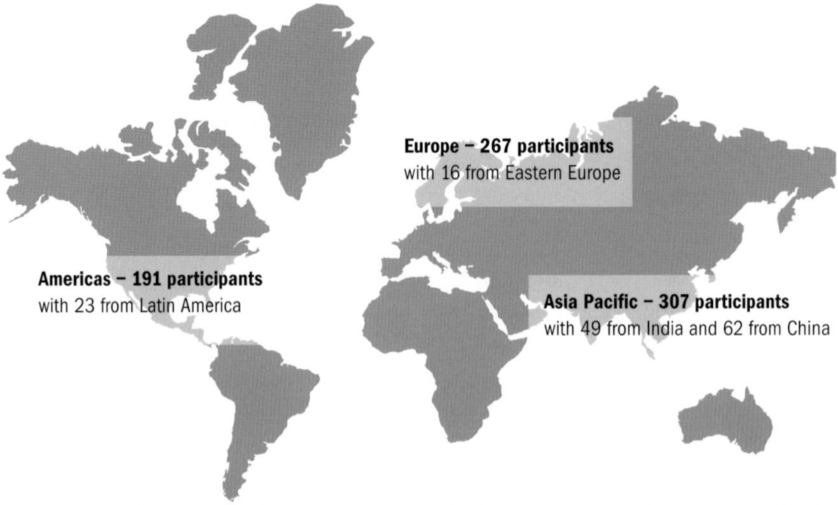

Europe – 267 participants
with 16 from Eastern Europe

Americas – 191 participants
with 23 from Latin America

Asia Pacific – 307 participants
with 49 from India and 62 from China

for which publicly reported financial information was available. For this subset, we compared their financial performance to that of an industry-accepted list of nearest competitors (up to 10 companies with similar revenue). Some of these competitors were *CEO Study* participants, but most were not.

By taking a five-year view, we were able to identify which companies outperformed or underperformed the average revenue growth, operating margin growth and historical operating margins of their closest competitors. Throughout our analysis, we used these top-half and bottom-half groupings to look for notable financial correlations. In this report, the term outperformers refers to the study participants in the top 50 per cent based on this competitive comparison, whereas underperformers are in the bottom 50 per cent. This financial analysis is of great interest because so few metrics are available to measure the impact of innovation, particularly innovation that goes beyond new products and services.

The three major themes that emerged from this study, described in detail below, are: business model innovation matters; external collaboration is indispensable; and innovation requires orchestration from the top.

> This financial analysis is of great interest because so few metrics are available to measure the impact of innovation, particularly innovation that goes beyond new products and services.

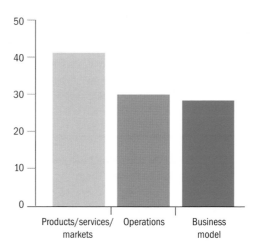

Figure 2. **CEOs' innovation emphasis.**
(Per cent of emphasis allocated to each innovation type)

Theme 1: Business Model Innovation Matters

Leaders frequently define their businesses in terms of the products and services they take to market and naturally focus their innovative energy there. But with technological advances and globalization presenting so many new opportunities – and threats – CEOs are now giving business model innovation as prominent a place on their agendas as products/services/markets

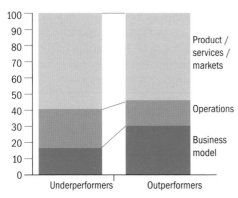

Figure 3. **Innovation priorities of underperformers versus outperformers.**
(Per cent of emphasis)

Note: Based on operating margin growth over five years as compared with competitive peers.

innovation and operational innovation (see Figure 2). As one CEO suggested, "the three areas are essential, equally important and inseparable from each other." Some CEOs who have not focused on business model innovation in the past now believe it is time.

While the fact that CEOs are now focusing almost 30 per cent of their innovation efforts on their business models is surprising, our financial analysis uncovered an even more interesting point. Companies whose operating margins have grown faster than competitors' were putting twice as much emphasis on business model innovation as underperformers (see Figure 3). Although business model innovation is clearly important to CEOs, it is part of a combination – which makes it critical to understand how CEOs have been managing each type of innovation. In the following sections, we share insights from CEOs – about motivating factors, specific innovation actions and anticipated benefits – that can inform other leaders as they construct and execute their own innovation agendas.

CEOs are using business model innovation to preempt threats – and to create them

Four out of every 10 business model innovators were afraid that changes in a competitor's business model would upset the competitive dynamics of the entire industry. One CEO described his predicament in dire terms: "Since 70 per cent of our business is based on a service that will no longer exist as we know it, we need to adapt our enterprise to survive."

If you have any doubts about the legitimacy of this fear or the dangers of waiting too long to change your business model, just think about the Eastman Kodak Company. It has been a wrenching process for the company to "wean itself" from the traditional film business (with its 60 per cent margins) and solidify its footing in the digital arena, with its stock price hitting a 20-year low in 2003.[1] But Kodak is focused on a business model turnaround. According to the company, 2005 marked the halfway point of its transformation, and it was also the first year in which Kodak's digital sales (at 54 per cent of total revenue) surpassed traditional revenue.[2]

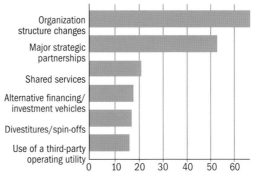

Figure 4. **Most common business model innovations.**
(Per cent of respondents)

Note: This question was asked of business model innovators only.

CEOs were candid about the need to search for new competitive differentiators – even if that meant confronting a sacrosanct business model. For example: "In the operations area, much of the innovation and cost savings that could be achieved have already been achieved. Our greatest focus is on business model innovation, which is where the greatest benefits lie." And: "It's not enough to make a difference on product quality or delivery readiness or production scale. We must innovate in areas where our competition does not act – by developing new competencies and alliances." Global connectivity (created through telecommunications, IT infrastructure and open standards) makes new skills and partners accessible and practical to employ. It enables entirely new forms of collaboration, and, thus, new business models. Of course, the same global connectivity also exposes firms to new competitors with very different business models and cost bases, which, in turn, can force business model innovation.

Instead of focusing on the threat, many of the CEOs we talked to described the top-line potential offered by business model changes. One CEO saw it as an absolute: "There's no growth without changing ourselves and the industry itself."

So, what actions are CEOs taking to adapt their business models? Major strategic partnerships and organization structural changes topped the list of most significant business model innovations (see Figure 4). One CEO explained that the success of strategic partnerships depends heavily on a company specializing and then working toward mutually beneficial value creation: "We need to develop a business model based on strategic partnerships that creates value not just for our company, but also for the industry as a whole. We cannot do everything in this era of specialization."

As global connectivity reduces transaction and collaboration costs, companies are taking advantage of the expertise and scale within their own organizations and across the globe. They are assembling a business model fashioned from groups of "specialized" capabilities – connecting internal expertise and scale through shared services centers with the capabilities of specialized partners to create truly differentiating business designs.[3]

Cost reduction and strategic flexibility were considered top benefits from business model innovation – being reported by over half of all business model innovators (see Figure 5). Business model innovation allows companies to specialize and move more quickly to seize emerging growth opportunities. Overall, CEOs' rankings suggest that business model innovation is helping their organizations become more

PARTNERS CAN BE INSTRUMENTAL

Porto Media is an example of a company that has relied on strategic partners to establish a totally new business model. The company had developed proprietary technology that enabled fast loading of digital content onto flash media cards. It envisioned a totally new business where customers could download music and movies onto these cards from kiosks at retail locations and play the content on compatible devices such as handheld players, phones or home media centers. The success of its new business model depended on two factors: Porto Media had to convince content providers that their content would be protected and used appropriately; and it needed a way to deliver that content to a network of retail locations.

Through collaboration with 4C (a consortium comprising Intel, IBM, Toshiba and Matsushita), Porto Media found a solution to its content protection dilemma. In response to requirements expressed by companies such as Porto Media, the consortium enhanced its Copy Protection for Recordable Media technology, creating the ability for content providers to specify flexible usage rules such as "play only once", "play until a certain date" or "play over a set time period". Porto Media combined its proprietary loading technology with the standards-based content protection technology developed by 4C into an attractive offer for content providers. Porto Media is also using a strategic partner to develop and manage the content delivery infrastructure at the core of its new business model.[4]

nimble and responsive, while at the same time lowering costs.

CEOs are making some fundamental changes to their organizations and business designs as part of their innovation initiatives. And an examination of their financial performance suggests why.

When we looked at financial performance over a five-year period, we found striking differences across the three types of innovation. Business model innovation had a much stronger correlation with operating margin growth than the other two types of innovation (see Figure 6). Examining the top actions of business model innovators, we found that companies innovating through strategic partnerships enjoyed the highest operating margin growth. As one CEO remarked, "reducing the cost base through cooperative models is important for any growth strategy."

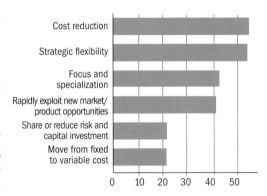

Figure 5. **Benefits cited by business model innovators.** *(Per cent of respondents)*

CEOs use operational innovation to drive much-needed efficiency

More than a few CEOs ranked operational innovation at the top of their priority lists, viewing it as a matter of survival. "We had such a large operating loss that we had to focus entirely on a financial turnaround," one said. High-cost, slow-responding, inefficient and antiquated are the adjectives CEOs used to describe the aspects of their operations that prompted them to concentrate on operational innovation. One CEO

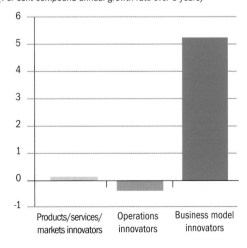

Figure 6. **Operating margin growth in excess of competitive peers.** *(Per cent compound annual growth rate over 5 years)*

stressed the enormity of past inefficiencies by labeling his enterprise's operation "a cross between a government agency and a church."

Though most CEOs still think of operations innovation as an efficiency play, others see it as dual-purpose. New-found efficiency and effectiveness not only allow them to control costs, but also help them to compete more formidably, gain market share and increase revenue. One CEO explained: "Although the main focus is strategically

A VARIABLE VIRTUAL COMPANY

Lam Research is making strategic partnerships fundamental to its overall business model, creating what it calls a "variable virtual company." Lam designs, manufactures, markets and services semiconductor processing equipment through more than 40 customer support centers in North America, Europe and Asia. In 2001, the company began shifting a significant portion of its costs to variable status through outsourcing. Today, it relies on partners for functions as diverse as HR, IT, finance and accounting, facilities management, customer service, indirect materials procurement, module engineering and manufacturing. In 2003, Lam extended its model by co-founding CapOneSource, a buying alliance that aggregates the buying power of a broad range of capital equipment companies, reducing each company's total outsourcing costs even further. Together, the members leverage common, standardized business processes based on the capabilities of "A-list" providers in each functional area. Lam's results have benefited from its innovative business model; it was among 26 companies chosen by *Forbes* in December 2005 for the prestigious "Best Managed Companies" list.[5]

on revenue generation, we first need to create the operational and technological foundation for that growth, so that product and customer strategies are sown on fertile ground."

Given this backdrop of motivations, operational innovators cited a variety of significant innovative actions which they had recently implemented. Although CEOs were pursuing a wide range of operational innovations, they were most focused on making their operations more responsive (see Figure 7).

The next two most frequent answers point to how they were achieving greater responsiveness – by automating processes and applying new science to persistent operational challenges.

Although we found the correlation between financial performance and operational innovation to be generally weaker than it was with business model innovation, this does not mean CEOs can afford to

TAGGING TOMATOES

As an Australian produce company that supplies supermarkets, fruit markets and national restaurant chains, Moraitis Fresh is keenly aware of rising demands for fresher produce. By placing radio frequency identification tags on tomato trays, the company can track the origin, packing date, type, quality and size of the tons of tomatoes it ships every day. Because it knows the precise amount and quality of tomatoes in its supply chain at any point in time, the company can respond rapidly to retailer requests for a specific volume and grade of tomato. The company can tell its retail customers exactly when and where the produce was grown, packed and shipped, which is particularly important as the world works toward food traceability and safer food supply chains. Improved information also allows Moraitis to pay growers based on the actual quality and number of tomatoes received (instead of by tonnage, regardless of grade).[6]

ignore the operational realm. The weaker correlation could indicate that operational innovation and products/services/markets innovation have become "table stakes" in the competitive game. Yet some aspects of operational innovation may still offer differentiated results. When we compared the financial performance of companies pursuing different categories of operational innovation, we found that companies that were making their operations more responsive to customers outperformed their competitors in terms of operating margins.

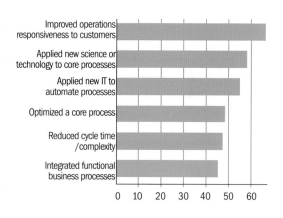

Figure 7. **Most common operations innovations.**
(Per cent of respondents)

Note: This question was asked of operations innovators only.

Products/services/markets innovation remains fundamental

In many industries – such as media, consumer goods and fashion – a regular stream of products/services/markets innovation is fundamental. "Innovation is our business," those CEOs explained. As one consumer goods CEO put it, "Last year's products are last

EXTENDING THE MARKET THROUGH INNOVATIVE SERVICES

Visa International CEMEA is leveraging the popularity of mobile phones to increase its share of the payment market and drive greater adoption of mobile payment solutions. For customers, the service is straightforward. After registering their Visa cards, mobile phone users can recharge airtime or pay their phone bills by simply sending a message from the handset. For operators, it is an attractive proposition as well. Visa, with help from technology partner Upaid, provides a standard platform that brings together multiple banks and operators in a local consortium in each market. As customers become more accustomed to making remote payments for mobile phone-related services, Visa expects to parlay this initial success into a wider range of payment applications.[7]

year's dollars." After all, products, services and markets form the core of the business. To sum up the prevailing view: "If you don't get your products, services and markets right, the other stuff doesn't matter."

Products/services/markets innovators have implemented a variety of innovation actions (see Figure 8). CEOs' attention was fairly evenly distributed, from market penetration to continuous product improvement to channel enablement. Overall, products/services as well as markets garnered more investment than channels. But priorities shifted as companies entered new markets or new customer segments. "Channels in our business are well established," one CEO said. "But as we target new geographic markets, we expect some scope of innovation on the channel front as well." CEOs also mentioned "developing multiple channels with different approaches for different customers."

As CEOs contemplate their innovation priorities, how much attention does innovation in products/services/markets warrant? In our financial analysis, we noted a positive correlation between products/services/markets innovation and above-average operating margins.

Figure 8. Most common products/services/markets innovations.
(Per cent of respondents)

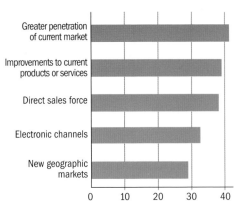

Note: This question was asked of products/services/markets innovators only.

Over a five-year period, products/ services markets innovators edged past competitors' operating margins by a little over 1 per cent.

Put in context, companies that are using business model innovation enjoyed significant operating margin growth, while those using products/services/markets and operational innovation have sustained their margins over time. If CEOs' emphasis on business model innovation continues (or intensifies), such innovation could become the relentless battleground that operational and products/services/ markets innovation represent today. For more on strategies for introducing effective business model innovations, see chapter 3, *Paths to success: Three ways to innovate your business model.*

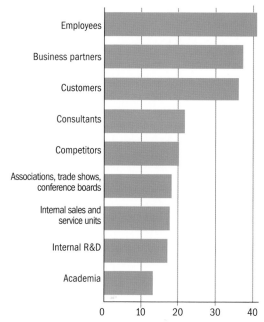

Figure 9. **Most significant sources of innovative ideas.** *(Per cent of respondents)*

Note: Respondents could select up to three choices.

Theme 2: External Collaboration is Indispensable

When asked which sources their companies relied on most for their innovative ideas, CEOs' responses held some surprises (see Figure 9). Business partners were right near the top of the list – just behind the general employee population. And customers were third. This means two of the three most significant sources of innovative ideas now lie outside the organization.

According to one CEO, "Some of the boldest plans under consideration within our company work by leveraging the collaborative potential of service providers in other domains." Speaking from the perspective of one of those partners, another CEO saw his firm as "the R&D arm" of its clients.

Internal R&D, on the other hand, was conspicuously buried much further down the list. Only 17 per cent of CEOs mentioned it.

WORKING WITH COMPETITORS

Always expected to provide the highest level of service at a reasonable cost, Xcel Energy is bringing together the innovative energies of several external partners in a proof-of-concept center it calls Utility Innovations. As part of this initiative, Xcel's strategic partners – some of which are competitors – are working together on innovations that leverage technology in new and different ways. The overall objectives are to increase customer satisfaction and reduce costs. Using this collaborative arrangement, Xcel pooled its resources with contributions from each partner to fund the innovation project. Initially, some of the partners were hesitant to work so closely with competitors, but decided that the advantages outweighed the intellectual property risks. The Utility Innovations project now gives partners access to a "real-world laboratory" (which happens to be one of their key clients), helps each partner make better product development decisions and encourages teamwork that transcends competitive boundaries.[8]

This middle-of-the-pack ranking is just one more indication that CEOs have expanded their innovation focus beyond products and services, and it raises a provocative question about what type of role R&D should be playing in operational and business model innovation.

External sources were not only prevalent in the ranking of CEOs' most significant sources of ideas, but they also comprised a substantial portion of the overall quantity of ideas. This trend was particularly evident among financial outperformers. Companies with higher revenue growth reported using external sources significantly more than slower growers. One CEO declared bluntly: "If you think you have all the answers internally, you are wrong."

When we examined extensive collaborators' responses by industry, the split between internal and external ideas appeared fairly even: 43 per cent of innovative ideas came from outside in the consumer packaged goods industry; 44 per cent in government and 42 per cent in industrial products. And externally generated ideas actually outnumbered internal ideas in two industries: 62 per cent in chemical and petroleum; and 54 per cent in telecommunications.

Our findings on sources of ideas coincide closely with CEOs' overall opinions about collaboration and partnering. Regardless of the type of innovation undertaken, more than 75 per cent of CEOs indicated that collaboration and partnering is very important to innovation. One CEO described its importance on a scale of one to five as "enormous": "I'd give this a six if I could."

But CEOs have a problem – and it is not a small one. Although collaborative aspirations were high, actual implementation was dramatically lower. Only half of the CEOs we spoke with believed their organizations were collaborating beyond a moderate level. As many CEOs explained, collaboration and partnering is "theoretically easy," but "practically hard to do." Whether it involves crossing internal or corporate boundaries, collaboration requires serious intent. As one CEO put it, "having a few beers together is not collaboration. Collaboration is a discipline."

When reflecting on this collaboration gap, CEOs spoke about lacking the skills and expertise needed to collaborate and partner externally. For one CEO, the market demands for collaboration had crept up on the organization, forcing it to be "reactive" rather than "strategic" in its partnering arrangements. In his own words, "it has been like Relationship 101 – we're terrible and we need to improve."

ENCOURAGING COLLABORATION INSIDE AND OUT

Novartis, the Swiss pharmaceutical company, is intent on bringing together internal and external expertise to create new market opportunities. Its organizational structure was specifically designed with "permeable boundaries" that make it easy for teams to work across disciplines, functions, geographies and corporate boundaries. To further its research and development efforts, the company routinely establishes strategic alliances with other industry players and academic institutions. Leaders are encouraged to cultivate external connections throughout the industry. A sterling example of the output from this type of collaborative approach is its leading cancer medication, Gleevec.[9]

Traditionally, cancer treatments attack both cancerous and healthy cells, leaving patients extremely weak. Counter to prevailing opinion at the time, a Novartis researcher believed it was possible to develop a drug that would target only unhealthy cells, thereby easing the burden on cancer patients. His external contacts at the Dana Farber Cancer Institute in Boston provided the pivotal clue he needed in his research, suggesting that such a treatment would most likely be effective against a specific type of cancer known as chronic myeloid leukemia. Later in the process, other external contacts helped identify hospitals for patient trials. And in the end, Gleevec enjoyed the fastest approval ever awarded by the U.S. Food and Drug Administration for a cancer drug. In 2005, it was the top-selling drug in its therapeutic category, with worldwide sales of $US2.2 billion. Through extensive collaboration, both internally and externally, Novartis has been able to build one of the strongest pipelines in the industry, with 76 drugs in some stage of clinical development.[10]

Despite all the potential challenges encountered when collaborating externally, some CEOs argued that internal collaboration sometimes proves even more difficult. In fact, the inability to collaborate internally can foil companies' attempts to deliver innovative value propositions for their clients.

For example, a large media conglomerate envisioned a new offering for its clients. With large-scale operations in network TV, cable TV, radio and the Internet, it hoped to capitalize on its scope by offering complex, integrated advertising deals that bundled together spots across multiple media formats, or "platforms." While advertisers were attracted by the simultaneous access to target audiences across these different formats, the executives responsible for the strategy had immense difficulty creating, selling and managing unified advertising deals because the operations of the individual platforms could not collaborate effectively. They had trouble gathering ratings data for audiences across platforms, creating common financial and contractual definitions and gaining agreement on pricing decisions from multiple sales managers. The disappointing result: slow response times, high error rates, senior managers burdened by administrative tasks – all culminating in little market success.

But in the area of operational innovation, public and private sector views diverged. Among the public sector leaders focused on operational innovation, more than 40 per cent considered themselves extensive collaborators – while only 18 per cent of the private sector operations innovators reported the same collaborative capabilities. Growing budget deficits, a greater focus on citizens as customers and government's adoption of leading commercial practices may be contributors to this higher degree of operational collaboration.

CEOs report unexpected benefits

CEOs described a broad spectrum of benefits from collaboration and partnering – both predictable and unexpected (see Figure 10). Cost reduction was clearly top of mind. But this was just a start. Moving down the list, the majority of benefits were actually drivers of top-line growth.

One CEO, for example, indicated that the higher customer satisfaction generated through collaboration ultimately resulted in more revenue: "In this commoditized market, we are able to command greater customer loyalty because of collaborative innovations. This implies both higher revenues and lower risks."

The upside of collaboration is underscored not only by qualitative CEO feedback, but also by the financial performance of companies with extensive collaboration capabilities. Extensive collaborators outperformed the competition in terms of both revenue growth and average operating margin. When we analyzed operating margin results, for example, more than half of the extensive collaborators outperformed their closest competitors (see Figure 11). There exists, however, a significant gap between the need for collaboration and the ability to do so, and this is clearly a significant roadblock to innovation that CEOs need to address. Moreover, since so many ideas come from outside, leaders need to pay particular attention to strengthening collaborative capabilities at the perimeters of their organizations, a topic explored in chapter 4, *The power of many: ABCs of collaborative innovation.*

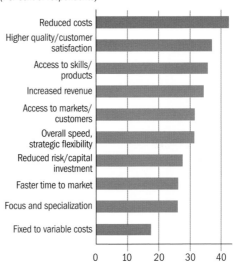

Figure 10. Collaboration and partnering benefits cited by CEOs.
(Per cent of respondents)

- Reduced costs
- Higher quality/customer satisfaction
- Access to skills/products
- Increased revenue
- Access to markets/customers
- Overall speed, strategic flexibility
- Reduced risk/capital investment
- Faster time to market
- Focus and specialization
- Fixed to variable costs

0   10   20   30   40

PUBLIC SECTOR LEADERS MORE CONFIDENT THAN PRIVATE SECTOR

Public sector leaders were key contributors to our *2006 CEO Study,* making up 14 per cent of our sample. Like their private sector counterparts, these leaders agree that collaboration is critical for all types of innovation. And both groups report a significant gap in their ability to collaborate and partner for both business model and products/services/markets innovation.

Overall, public sector leaders exhibited a general sense of accomplishment in the operations arena, with the majority now giving highest priority to products/services/markets innovation (ranking it even higher than the private sector did). One leader explained it this way: "We are at the point in the agency's development where we have achieved savings by doing things better; now we want to do better things."

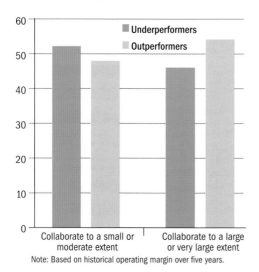

Figure 11. Use of collaboration among underperformers and outperformers.
(Per cent of respondents)

Note: Based on historical operating margin over five years.

Theme 3: Innovation Requires Orchestration from the Top

In case there was any doubt about whose responsibility it is to foster innovation, CEOs cleared that up quickly. Their most frequent response was: "I am."

The second most frequent answer, "no specific individual," essentially reflected the same sentiment. The responsibility was simply too big to rest on one person's shoulders – unless it was their own. "Leading, setting direction, laying the cultural groundwork that stimulates innovation – it's essential work for a CEO," acknowledged one executive. (Noticeably absent was any sizable mention of R&D, with fewer than 3 per cent of CEOs suggesting that the general manager of R&D was responsible for innovation.)

However, leading their organizations to be more innovative is becoming more difficult. As massive change bears down, employees, stockholders and boards are increasingly impatient for results. And when those results are not forthcoming, the consequences can be severe. Nearly half of *Fortune 1000* CEOs have been replaced since 2000 (with a record-breaking turnover of 129 CEOs in 2005).[11]

One CEO used a golf analogy to describe how innovation leadership should work: "I am responsible for showing the team where the green is, establishing a broad fairway and supplying them with a good range of clubs. I then give them the freedom to decide how best to play the hole." But in reality, many CEOs experience difficulty in getting employees to act: "Employees behave as if it is inappropriate to rock the boat." And some employees simply abdicate responsibility to the person in charge. "Innovation czar equals innovation ghetto," according to one CEO.

Looking through CEOs' top 10 innovation obstacles, it is apparent that the majority of issues reside somewhere inside their own organizations. Culture, budget, people and process were cited as

Figure 12. **Most significant obstacles to innovation.**
(Per cent of respondents)

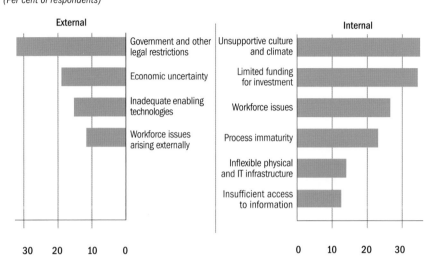

some of the most significant hurdles (see Figure 12). For CEOs, this is a classic case of "good news, bad news." Because the issues are internal, CEOs have more control over them. However, these hurdles compound the challenge CEOs face.

CEOs instinctively understand the need to play a prominent role in establishing an innovative culture. But they are not always certain how to go about it. Our findings suggest two major factors can help CEOs orchestrate greater innovative achievements:

• A culture that is collegial and team-oriented, but still rewards individual contributions; and

• More consistent integration of business and technology.

A collegial culture with individual rewards

The majority of CEOs described their creativity cultures as highly collaborative, collegial and team-oriented – as opposed to being focused on individuals or predominantly confined to specific subgroups. It is also worth noting that companies in which the CEO orchestrates a more team-oriented culture were decidedly more profitable than organizations with segregated pockets of innovators (see Figure 13).

Although a team-oriented environment is critical, 77 per cent of the

INSPIRING IDEAS THROUGH FRIENDLY DEBATE

Google is well known for creating search capabilities that have changed the way individuals and organizations use the Internet. But behind the tools many take for granted every day are 5000 collaborators working on more great ideas. In Google's "networked" model, ideas and data are king. Employees are encouraged to initiate dialogue and debate new concepts, whether it be via email "ideas mailing lists," the company intranet or face-to-face. Google favors a flatter organizational structure with a relatively high ratio of line employees to managers (20:1, compared to an industry average of 7:1), giving employees access to more information and, consequently, more power. A sense of community and collective pride permeate its California office. With the exception of a few dozen executives, all employees share cubicles. Tasks are typically tackled by small teams. Two guiding principles help Google "foster useful conflict and make fast decisions": All suggestions must be backed up by data; and no concept can be deemed "stupid."[12]

CEOs we interviewed agreed that it was also important to recognize significant contributions made by individuals. Our analysis also noted a financial correlation associated with this choice. While many factors can contribute to financial performance, companies that reward individual contributions achieved 2 per cent higher operating margins on average and increased revenue nearly 3 per cent faster than those that did not.

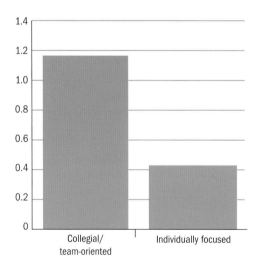

Figure 13. **Margin performance associated with cultural approach.**
(Per cent of historical five-year average operating margin in excess of peers)

Business and technology integration

CEOs view business and technology integration as vital to innovation – or as one CEO put it, "as important as water is for sea traffic." Because of the unprecedented pace and breadth of technological change, CEOs realize its strategic impact on all areas of the business.

Most saw these advances as

opportunity. They spoke of technology enabling "daring ideas" – a way to consolidate physical offices into virtual ones, to discover customer insights that drive product and brand extensions, to spot emerging trends that competitors miss. One CEO described how his organization avoids being blind-sided: "We get involved early on, in infancy ... across a range of technologies relevant to our capabilities and the needs of our customers. We maintain a portfolio of technologies, never knowing for certain which technology will take off next, but always having a hand in as many relevant areas as we can identify."

Nearly 80 per cent of the CEOs we interviewed rated business and technology integration as being of great importance. But, as was the case with collaboration, CEOs have a major "integration gap". The lack of integration frustrated many CEOs. They wanted to improve, but "didn't know how to do it" or found the task "too complicated." For others, the gap loomed large because of latent potential. One CEO expressed the chase this way: "Even more is still possible ... and feasible. We cannot do enough!"

For the subset of CEOs who have gone further, integrating business and technology beyond moderate levels, it has paid off. Extensive integrators were much more enthusiastic about the benefits they were receiving than the less integrated (see Figure 14). Though cost reduction topped the list, the bulk of the benefits actually relates to driving top-line revenue. CEOs who had implemented more extensive

AN OFFER CUSTOMERS CAN'T REFUSE

Expensive long-distance phone charges spelled opportunity for Skype. Matching this market need with Voice over Internet Protocol (VoIP) technology, the company was able to offer communication capabilities at a fraction of the price most customers were paying. Rather than using phone lines to connect callers (or a centralized computer server to track calls, like previous VoIP providers), Skype relies on Internet connections to carry voice, messages and, most recently, live footage of the person at the other end of the line. By using existing Internet connections, Skype can offer these services for a low fee. Introduced in 2003 with no advertising, Skype's popularity grew by word of mouth, with customers eager to take advantage of low-cost phone services. Registered users numbered 74 million as of early 2006, and the company was purchased by eBay in 2005 for about $US2.6 billion in cash and stock.[13]

business and technology integration reported greater customer satisfaction, speed and flexibility.

In fact, extensive integrators reported revenue increases three times as often as companies that were less integrated. These views correspond to our own financial comparisons: we found that extensive integrators were increasing revenue 5 per cent faster than their competitors.

To summarise the leadership theme, CEOs must drive the changes required to create an innovative culture. Leading innovation requires an unwavering commitment to a team-oriented environment that also recognizes outstanding individual contributions, and business and technology integration that is implemented across the organization. In chapter 5, *The Lean Six Sigma way: Driving operational innovation,* we show how Lean Six Sigma methods, and the cultivation of Lean Six Sigma experts throughout an organization, can foster a climate of continuous and widespread innovation. In chapter 6, *The new rules of Value 2.0: How to capitalize on emerging technologies,* we describe the power that can be harnessed by using emerging technologies in what is sometimes called Web 2.0, technologies that are poised to launch a whole new era of collaboration.

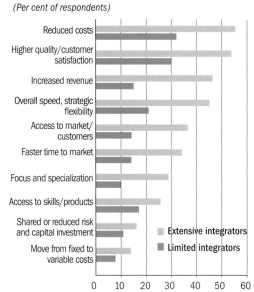

Figure 14. Benefits cited by extensive integrators versus limited integrators.
(Per cent of respondents)

The Innovation Horizon

Our conversations with CEOs leave no doubt: globalization and technology advances are greatly intensifying competition while creating unprecedented opportunities to differentiate. Financial markets are demanding ever-faster growth. Growth – and perhaps even survival – depends on innovation.

Unlike invention, which comes from effort, experimentation and, at times, an element of luck, innovation relies more on skill and leadership

– choosing the best places to focus innovative attention and creating the ideal environment for innovation to flourish. Yes, the creative spark will always play a role, but CEOs must also find ways to make innovation happen more systematically. As when implementing a corporate strategy, becoming more innovative means making deliberate choices – filtering the plethora of options you have as a CEO and concentrating on those few actions that can truly make a difference. As is so often the case in business, the key differentiator is execution.

Distilling the collective thinking of 765 corporate and public sector leaders, what emerges is a much clearer picture of what innovation requires and which leadership actions matter. Based on these insights, we offer several actions you can take to expand your own innovation agenda.

Think broadly, act personally, manage the mix of innovation

- Has your innovation agenda expanded beyond products/services/markets innovation and operational improvement to encompass your business model – the emerging basis for competition?
- Do you know which innovations you are investing in – and which you are not?
- How much of your innovation is bold versus routine?

When it comes to innovation, many CEOs still fall back on their traditional comfort zone: products/services/markets. But business model innovation is becoming more critical to compete and grow.

To orchestrate greater levels of innovation, you will need to develop and manage a bold innovation strategy that spans all three types of innovation – products/services/markets, operations and, most importantly, business model innovation. Make sure the combination of efforts helps you create a truly differentiated business model that delivers superior value to customers and distinguishes you from competitors. Set the scope and the pace of innovation, and then make sure the organization accepts the responsibility to drive its success.

Make your business model deeply different

- How vulnerable is your business model? Are you playing in the right place in your networked industry value chain?
- How would your business model be different if you started with a

clean sheet of paper? What would you do if you were getting into your current business as a start-up located in Malaysia?

- What capabilities do you have that might fundamentally change the value chain in another industry?

Given the potential impact of business model innovation, it is critical to take a close look at your business to identify the few essential elements or components that set you apart – and find innovative ways to obtain the rest. Consider options far beyond basic shared services centers, outsourcing or insourcing – for instance, partnering with a competitor to gain a mutual advantage over the rest of the industry, or participating in a common, industry-wide utility that lowers everyone's costs. Consider new approaches to defining and evaluating the components of your business, their strategic value and how best to implement them.

Look for ways to transform your core value proposition. Pay particular attention to ignored areas of the value chain where no one is actively innovating. Search out third parties that could add value or technology that could introduce new ways of doing business.

Do not focus on business model innovation simply because you believe there is a threat to your business. Concentrate instead on the opportunities – they typically outweigh the threats. Besides, the business model innovation you pursue does not need to be in your own core business; it could be a new business opportunity in another industry. Regardless of your motivation and where you look for opportunities, choose business model innovations that make you deeply different.

Ignite innovation through business and technology integration

- Do you continuously explore new technologies that could change your business? Is technological change an input to your strategy development process?
- What are you doing to maintain or recreate an entrepreneurial atmosphere in which business and technology integration occur naturally?
- Are you shaping the technology agenda in your industry or following it?

Technology can be a catalyst – both to drive innovation and to enable it. It can play a vital part in new products, services, channels, market-entry strategies, operational transformation and industry-altering business models. Technology can even facilitate other innovation enablers such as collaboration.

But capitalizing on all this potential requires combining business and market insights with technological know-how.[14] This happens inherently in a start-up endeavor because the entrepreneur is the embodiment of integration. But if you are past those early stages, you have to drive it differently. Business and market needs and opportunities should be evaluated in concert with technological possibilities – and this needs to happen early, when strategies are first being developed.

Over time, technologies can become so ingrained in day-to-day operations that continued use and investment happens by default rather than by explicit choice. Before you can evaluate the impact that new technologies or changes in technology investment might have on profitability, you may need to take a step back and ascertain which existing technology investments are aligned with which business operations and which products/services. Understanding the alignment can help you make better decisions about future investments.

Defy collaboration limits

- How effectively do different product, geography and functional teams really collaborate in your organization? What results have you realized from this?
- How have you used collaboration to promote the sharing of best practices and ultimately to create specialized capabilities in your organization?
- What could you accomplish if you learned radical lessons from other sectors?

We now have tools to work together to shape, develop and move ideas forward faster than ever before. Work can be reconfigured in totally new ways with less regard for when and where it is done, and who does it. Skill and scale can finally come together. As scattered specialists link up and collaborate, you may uncover a new, differentiated capability that you would never have imagined if those experts continued to work in isolation.

Collaboration on a massive, geography-defying scale literally opens a world of possibilities for the way products, services, processes and business models are (re)designed and implemented. Distance, scale, language, company walls – limits that once seemed immutable are now broken on a regular basis.

BEYOND COLLABORATION BOUNDARIES

Collaboration does not have to be limited by sheer numbers, company payroll or physical proximity. InnoCentive, for example, brings together 85,000 scientists located in more than 175 countries to work on seemingly intractable scientific challenges, multiplying the brainpower of participating companies such as Boeing, Dow Chemical, Eli Lilly and Procter & Gamble.[15]

Goldcorp Inc. used a contest to attract external collaborators. It posted geological data for one of its high-grade gold mines on the Web, challenging the world's geologists to find gold. Some 1400 prospectors from 51 countries responded, and the company drilled the first four of the winners' top five targets and struck gold on each one. The winning geologists never even visited the mine.[16]

Even physical collaboration no longer depends on being in the same location. In 2005, Australian scientists performed microsurgery on cells located on the other side of the world in California.[17]

Collaborating on a massive scale can also involve computing power, not just brainpower. The World Community Grid is using aggregated capacity from more than 270,000 devices volunteered by individuals and organizations to study human proteome folding and design new anti-HIV drugs.[18]

Often, the only remaining barrier is fear. And that is where you may need to start. Be clear about which ostensible barriers are impeding collaboration. Question their legitimacy. The limits may be in our minds.

Force an outside look ... every time

- How often do you turn outside for innovation? To whom?
- Are your partnering agreements designed to encourage innovative contributions – or are they just focused on cutting costs?
- Have you designed your customer-facing processes to solicit ideas and act on insights that come from direct customer interaction?

Left alone, most teams will attempt to solve problems internally. It is familiar territory; it is where they are most comfortable. As a leader, your role is to force the outside look, pushing the organization to work with outsiders more than insiders. As you examine new product or service concepts, plans for new markets, operational and business model adjustments, ask where the external contribution is (or why it is missing). And don't ease up too soon. Even companies that have had tremendously successful external collaboration and partnering initiatives often fall back on old insular habits.

Consider inviting CEOs and other senior executives from other industries to look at your business from a fresh angle. You might even offer to return the favor, and in doing so, double your learning opportunities.

Conclusion

Two out of every three CEOs we interviewed said they need to drive fundamental change within their organizations over the next two years. To no one's surprise, CEOs recognised a profound need to innovate in order to achieve this change. But this study gives us a richer view of how leaders are driving that innovation. We see that the innovation mix matters – and that business models should be prime targets for innovation. We understand how collaboration, partnering and technology integration are inexorably linked to innovation – and which areas of weakness need to be addressed quickly. And we are confronted with the truth that CEOs must personally orchestrate innovation, establishing conditions that ignite innovative ideas and driving their execution.

The CEOs who participated in our study are eyeing a much wider innovation horizon. They are poised to seize opportunities. And we are hopeful that the innovative momentum building in these 765 organizations and their peers around the globe will spill over into solutions for our world – innovations that help us feed, care for and fuel a planet that may well have more than 8 billion people by 2030.[19] Think big and bold. Our future depends on it.

References

1 Kher, Unmesh. "Getting Kodak to Focus." *Time*. February 7, 2005. http://www.time.com/time/insidebiz/printout/0,8816,1025191,00.html

2 "Kodak's 4th-Quarter Sales Rise 12% to $4.197 Billion." Kodak press release. January 30, 2006. http://www.kodak.com/eknec/PageQuerier.jhtml?pq-path=2709&pq-locale=en_US&gpcid=0900688a8048b92f

3 Pohle, George, Peter Korsten, Shanker Ramamurthy and Steven Foecking. "The specialized enterprise: A fundamental redesign of firms." November 2005. http://www-1.ibm.com/services/us/index.wss/ibvstudy/imc/a1009224?cntxt=a1000401

4 "Porto Media speeds time to market with standards-based solution." IBM case study. February 2006. http://www-1.ibm.com/services/us/index.wss/casestudy/imc/a1023486?cntxt=a1000062

[5] Described with permission from IBM client; "Forbes Names Lam Research Corporation a 'Best Managed' Company Among 'Platinum 400: Best Big Companies in America'." Lam Research press release. January 4, 2006.

[6] "Moraitis Fresh's RFID implementation improves productivity and retailer relationships." IBM case study. April 2005. http://www-306.ibm.com/software/success/cssdb.nsf/CS/GJON-68S3DG?OpenDocument&Site=default

[7] "Visa International CEMEA extends innovative mobile payment solution." January 13, 2004. http://www.upaid.net/press_release_det.asp?art_id=2867&sec_id=581; "Mobile operators across Central & Eastern Europe, Middle East & Africa (CEMEA) sign up to Visa's Mobile Service." July 6, 2005. http://www.upaid.net/Press_Release_det.asp?id=3059&sec_id=581

[8] "How to 'Xcel' at Technology-Driven Business Innovation." Energy Insights, "In the Know" newsletter. June 20, 2005; "Chartwell's Best Practices for Utilities and Energy Companies." Volume 7, No 7, July 2005.

[9] Cross, Rob, Jeanne Liedtka and Leigh Weiss. "A Practical Guide to Social Networks." *Harvard Business Review*. March 2005.

[10] "Novartis delivers strong performance with record results in 2005." Novartis International AG investor relations release. http://www.novartis.com/downloads_new/investors/Q4%202005%20REPORT%20-%20ENGLISH%20-%20FINAL_CORRECTED.pdf

[11] "Record-breaking CEO Churn in 2005." Burson Marsteller press release. January 31, 2006. http://www.burson-marsteller.com/pages/news/releases/2006/press-1-31-2006

[12] Hardy, Quentin. "Google Thinks Small." *Forbes*. November 14, 2005. http://www.forbes.com/execpicks/global/2005/1114/054A.html

[13] "New model networks." *Management Today*. February 7, 2006. http://www.clickmt.com/public/news/index.cfm?fuseaction=fulldetails&newsUID=50dc8c4f-d4e5-4b9e-862b-f039f3e648e4; "Young upstarts are ringing the changes in telephony." *Computing*. February 2, 2006; Sullivan, Mark. "Skype's Still Talking to Itself." February 7, 2006. http://www.lightreading.com/document.asp?doc_id=87839&WT.svl=news1_1; "eBay to Acquire Skype." eBay press release. September 12, 2005. http://investor.ebay.com/downloads/eBay_PressRelease.pdf

[14] McCurry, Kevin, Saul J. Berman and Jeff Hagan. "Eliminating the strategic blind spot: Technology-driven business strategy spurs innovation and growth." March 21, 2005. http://www-1.ibm.com/services/us/index.wss/ibvstudy/imc/a1009225?cntxt=a1000401

[15] "Dr. Alpheus Bingham, InnoCentive's President and CEO, Receives 'Business Processes Award' at *The Economist's* Fourth Annual Innovation Summit." InnoCentive press release. November 30, 2005. http://www.innocentive.com/about/press/20051130_DrWinAward.html

[16] "US$575,000 Goldcorp Challenge Awards World's First 6 Million Ounce Internet Gold Rush Yields High Grade Results!" Goldcorp Inc. press release. March 12, 2001. http://www.goldcorpchallenge.com/challenge1/mediaclips/media_frameset.html; "Toronto, Ontario's Gold-corp Inc. launched the Internet gold rush..." Innovation in Canada. http://www.innovation.gc.ca/gol/innovation/stories.nsf/vengss/ss01056e.htm

[17] Jaques, Robert. "Doctors perform surgery over the Web." vnunet.com. August 9, 2005. http://www.vnunet.com/vnunet/news/2140922/internet-link-remote

[18] World Community Grid. http://www.worldcommunitygrid.org. Statistics: By Members. http://www.worldcommunitygrid.org/stat/viewMembers.do

[19] "World Population: 1950 to 2050." U.S. Census Bureau. April 2005. http://www.census.gov/ipc/www/img/worldpop.gif

Acknowledgments

This study is the result of extensive collaboration and partnering – well beyond the walls of IBM. And we would like to thank the many individuals who have contributed to this endeavor. Above all, we appreciate the 765 CEOs, business executives, and public sector leaders around the world who generously shared hours of time and years of experience with us. Their insights and enthusiasm made our study possible – and invaluable. We would also like to thank the hundreds of IBM Global Business Services partners and IBM client executives who conducted the in-person interviews and the Economist Intelligence Unit for its assistance with telephone interviews.

Without the leadership of our Executive Champions, Ginni Rometty and Doug Elix, this study would have remained just an innovative idea. The knowledge, guidance and direction provided by the CEO Study Executive Sponsors – Saul Berman, Marc Chapman, Steven Davidson, Martin Fleming, Peter Korsten, Rainer Mehl, Kristen Pederson and George Pohle – have been essential and integral to the success of this study. The Global CEO Study core team contributed to the study in countless ways – from study concept, survey instrument design, fielding and interview management, to data management and analysis as well as overall program management and marketing and deployment. Its members include: Steve Abruzzi, Denise Arnette, Steve Ballou, Ragna Bell, Amy Blitz, Lisa Buckley, Angie Casey, Erin Crapser, Niels Feldmann, Don Gordon, Christine Maehrle, Ankit Patel, Angela Suttie and Jim Turoff. Also deserving special mention are the IBM Survey Research Center for its deep survey and analytics knowledge as well as its technical assistance; the IBM Benchmarking Program for expertly managing the collection of survey data; and the IBM Institute for Business Value Research Center for its analytical and content development support.

Finally, we wish to thank the innumerable IBM colleagues worldwide who have supported this effort in some way. Their commitment to innovation – for our clients and for our company – has been amply demonstrated.

"Constant reinvention is the central necessity at GE ... We're all just a moment away from commodity hell."

Jeffrey Immelt, Chairman and CEO

Schonfeld, Erick. "GE Sees the Light By learning to manage innovation: Jeffrey Immelt is remaking America's flagship industrial corporation into a technology and marketing powerhouse." Business 2.0. July 1, 2004.

Speaking of innovation 1

RICHARD FLORIDA is one of the world's leading public intellectuals on economic competitiveness, demographic trends and cultural and technological innovation. He is Professor of Business and Creativity at the Rotman School of Management, University of Toronto. Previously, he held professorships at George Mason University and Carnegie Mellon University and taught as a visiting professor at Harvard and MIT. His books include *The Rise of the Creative Class* and *The Flight of the Creative Class*. His next book, *Who's Your City?*, is due out in March 2008.

Q: What kind of shift in thinking is required to create a sustainable culture of innovation? And what are the most effective strategies?
A: It's a big shift because for so long corporations have viewed innovation as being about once-in-a-lifetime astounding breakthroughs – the phrase people used to use was "creating the new nylon." And they thought they could have a group of innovators who would magically come up with The Big New Thing. And many companies, especially multinationals, and especially US multinationals, believed they could sequester all of these really smart people in a laboratory or R&D center.

But today they need to understand that innovation is continuous and that it happens everywhere. So more likely than not the things you need to be aware of are not happening in your R&D lab or in your sequestered little space. They're happening all around you and, in the words of my former Carnegie Mellon colleague Wes Cohen, you must have the absorptive capacity to integrate them very quickly.

So an important shift is occurring in the way we think about innovation. Human beings are particularly good at something much broader than innovation, something I just call creativity. And what you're talking about is mobilizing this continuous creativity across the organization and looking for it outside the organization. And that requires a quantum shift in the nature of the company. Because even a cursory reading of psychology tells you that creative people are motivated from within – they seek challenge and excitement and they seek to work on great projects. And if you don't give them that, if you think you can motivate them just with money, if you think you can make them meet timetables using only rules and money (the traditional tools for motivating people), they'll leave.

While companies like Google, Apple and IBM certainly understand this, a great example of a creative company is Toyota. Yes, it has fabulous R&D staff. And it has the fabulous product engineers who developed new hybrid cars and new battery technology. But the heart and soul of its innovation is in the creativity of its factory floor workers and in the creativity of its supply chain. It's about mobilizing creativity up from the factory floor and all the way through the supply chain. It's about harnessing and tapping the creative energy of tens of thousands of people. That's really the challenge for companies in the 21st century: How do you integrate the creativity that goes on in the factory floor, in the supply chain, in the design shop, and in the research lab? How do you mobilize that continuously?

Q: What are the biggest obstacles to building an innovative and creative corporate culture?
A: The first obstacle is the way we recruit people. Generally companies assess people by personality. They're looking for people who are conscientious and agreeable, who fit into the organization, and maybe in sales they're looking for extroverts. Yet psychological research shows that creative people tend to be open to experience. They like new ideas, and they like constant external stimulation. But they're not necessarily agreeable; they don't work well under timetables; they don't really much like being around other people. They certainly don't like rules, or feeling hemmed in. So if a company wants to be a creative organization, its managers have to find a way to integrate these strange people they've tended to shun. That's what the Silicon Valley companies like Apple and Google have done well. It's also what arts communities have always done well. The creative organization can't be rule-driven, and it has to deal with people who seem odd.

Secondly, it must get over the idea that only money motivates people. It has to understand that intrinsic rewards are critical. And–Peter

Drucker said this really well – in the information or knowledge-based age, you have to treat people as if they're volunteers whose commitment to your organization is contingent. Jim Goodnight at the SAS Institute told me, "My assets come through the gate at 9am and leave at 5pm and I have to convince them to come back again the next day, or they'll go somewhere else to work. And the way I do that is by challenging them." And those challenges are idiosyncratic.

The third thing is that you have to eliminate the hassles in people's lives. So much of our working day is spent dealing with minutiae – not just organisational bureaucracy but personal stuff too. If organizations want to mobilize creativity, they have to create a support structure for creative people, which means taking that stuff off people's shoulders. Jim and the SAS Institute did this by having on-site day care and schools and health-care facilities, and it makes sense. It doesn't mean doing every trendy, faddy thing, like putting an Ultimate Frisbee field in the cafeteria. If it doesn't add to the bottom line, if it doesn't mobilize human creativity, don't do it.

But the most important obstacles in organizations today are the squelchers. Jane Jacobs, the great urbanist, was one of my mentors. I remember asking her about the failure of cities to rejuvenate. Why do some cities fail to create interesting, artistic, musical neighbourhoods? Or fail to attract and retain college graduates? And you could ask similar questions about the failure of companies to be creative.

She replied that every city has creativity in its DNA, just as every organization has creativity within it. The reason it fails to win out is a group of people she called the squelchers. They're the people saying, "We're not doing it that way." Or: "It can't be done." Or: "Go somewhere else." And the least successful organizations are where the squelchers have the upper hand. There is a great struggle between the human urge to be creative and the counter-urge to control. And that control mentality is deeply ingrained in industrial-age organizations. In his new book, Gary Hamel says that our management systems have become literally inhuman. Those systems – which were so great for the industrial revolution – were about optimising the flow of physical goods and physical labor. They're not the kind of humanizing systems that motivate people. The word I use is that they've become prisons. And increasingly the organizations that function like prisons aren't going to attract people.

And so we come to a huge challenge for the modern organization: talented and creative people – we're not talking about lower skilled people with fewer opportunities – have so many options that they can more or less go where they choose. They can go to the location they choose, and ironically they're all picking similar places. So a company has to pick its location carefully. And many of the locations that were great for industrial-age companies don't really work for this creative age.

Also, you may need to be in multiple locations. Microsoft's decision to open a laboratory in Vancouver is very interesting. When the U.S. made it harder to get visas and therefore to work at Microsoft's Redmond headquarters outside Seattle, Vancouver became a way for Microsoft to access another talent pool. So that location – which wasn't picked for that reason – becomes incredibly useful.

So location is not a minor element of business strategy. Where you choose to locate is incredibly important to your corporate competitiveness because as well as competitive advantage, which you create, there's place-based advantage, which your community creates. And leveraging between them is really important.

Q: In *The Rise of the Creative Class* you wrote about the international competition to develop more robust ways of cultivating creativity. So who is doing it well today?
A: American companies still lead the world in this. And Toyota is still the best example of a truly creative company, a company that harnesses creative capacity throughout the organization. But good examples are becoming more widespread. And I think we make a mistake when we look at corporate and international competitiveness if we focus only on India and China. They have certainly taken great strides. But I think that the creative age is one in which smallness can be an advantage – where a small organization, a start-up can grow quickly. Also, smaller jurisdictions cannot be counted out. If you ask me which locations I see as innovative centers, then sure I think Shanghai and Bangalore are key

places, but certainly not all of India and China. I would list Sydney and Melbourne, and Stockholm and Copenhagen, and Amsterdam. And certainly some of the Canadian centers. And the reason is that as the US becomes harder to get into, people are not going to mass migrate to China or India. The mass migration of creative and talented people is going to occur to places that are open, cosmopolitan, and where English is the language of business.

And one of the key factors that companies have to understand – and I think they do – is that the innovation and creative system is becoming global. In the competitive world of the 1970s every nation had its competitive companies, which were kind of walled-off from one another. Then globalisation came along. And soon the auto industry became a global competition, and electronics and steel and so on. The same thing is now happening to the creative centers in cities. So if every country had 10 or 20 communities, now the world is being structured around 25-40 places. So the world is not only becoming a competitive platform for multinational companies, but for multinational centers of innovation. If you had a map that overlaid the two, that would be extremely interesting. Companies have to be thinking about that map. Global companies have to be in the 25-40 locations that really matter to global creativity and innovation.

Q: Are you optimistic about the outcome of the confrontation between the creative class and the squelchers?
A: So many people on the left whose sympathies are in the right place are looking for the return of hierarchical systems. Basically unions and workers thought they could secure seniority and job protection based around the hierarchy. So people think their status, their life and their identity are attached to this organization. Bupkes! For millennia people worked in small organic communities; the hierarchical organization is maybe 500 years old and it reached its zenith in the industrial age. Now we have to unlearn that. I remain incredibly optimistic and what gives me optimism is that for the first time in human history the logic of economic growth presupposes further human development. We will not prosper, we will not grow if we don't further develop our people – their creativity, their mental labor, their intellects. So I think we're in an interlude, a time of adjustment. If I had to periodize it in terms of the Industrial

Revolution, then I'd say we're the Industrial Revolution before Frederick Taylor. We're at the very dawn of this age. And most people who are managers today bear the genetic blueprint of living in the prison. It's going to take two generations, but the next two generations will completely rethink the system. When I hear Brad Anderson at Best Buy say "we have to move to corporate creativity, we have to be more like Toyota," that gives me great hope.

The other factor is the politics of the moment. People are very scared by the dawn of this new age. If you don't have the required skills, if you don't know technology, if you're afraid you're going to be displaced, then you want to go backwards. So the politics of this are the politics of fear and anxiety and that's reinforcing the hierarchy. Over a couple of generations, this will change, but it's not going to be automatic. It's going to take a long time and a lot of hard work to institutionalize the new way of doing business. But the places that do it will win and the companies that do it will win. And a Darwinian process will weed out the hierarchical losers.

Paths to success

Three ways to innovate your business model

Edward Giesen, Saul Berman,
Ragna Bell and Amy Blitz

Innovation in business models is a success differentiator
for CEOs. We identified three main types of business model
innovation: the industry model, the revenue model and the
enterprise model. We then compared these types across
35 best practice cases and found that each one, used alone or
in combination and with the right strategy and strong execution,
can bring success. But enterprise model innovation emphasizing
external collaboration and partnerships is the most common.

The ability of CEOs to shift direction and introduce business
model innovations in a rapidly changing global business environment
is proving to be a critical success factor. In fact, the *Expanding the
Innovation Horizon* found that business model innovation had a
much stronger correlation with operating margin growth than other
types of innovation.[1] But what exactly is business model innovation?
And which type yields the best results? Neither the CEOs we spoke
with nor a review of the current literature provided a clear response.

FIGURE 1. **Profit outperformers focus on business model innovation more frequently than underperformers.**

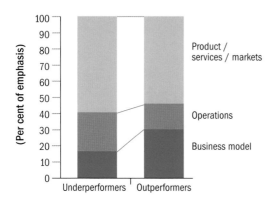

Note: Based on operating margin growth over five years as compared to competitive peers.
Source: "*Expanding the Innovation Horizon: The Global CEO Study 2006,*" IBM Global Business Services. March 2006.

So we set out to find an answer. In our research, we identified three main types of business model innovation, which can be used alone or in combination – innovations in industry models, in revenue models and in enterprise models. We then compared these types across 35 best practice cases. In this chapter, we demonstrate that each type, with the right strategy and strong execution, can generate success.

While each of the three types of business model innovation can lead to success, we found that innovations in enterprise models that focus on network plays (that is, external collaboration and partnerships) are the most common, with 15 of the 35 cases we studied using this type of business model innovation. Moreover, we found that companies using network plays realized similar financial results to companies that used other strategies. We also found that while network plays are being used by diverse companies in different industries and regions, and of varying age, size and other characteristics, this tactic has been particularly useful for older companies.

So when it comes to business model innovation, many paths may lead to success, with collaboration and network plays being the most common approach. The key is to seize opportunity in new ways to better meet customer needs using strategies that fit the overall strengths and vision of the organization. Strong execution must then follow.

Business model innovation matters

Today's CEOs face tremendous opportunities, as well as threats, from various directions. Consider the Internet. While it may seem like old news these days, the Internet is one factor that continues to transform the global business environment. Relatively recent entrants like Google, MySpace and YouTube, to name but a few, are demonstrating the power to introduce disruptive business model innovations using the Internet.

Clearly, there is substantial opportunity to leverage that power to create new industries and reinvent existing ones. Add to this the rise of China, India, Russia, Brazil and other emerging markets, and the sense of both opportunities and threats for CEOs, not to mention confusion, grows.

In the *IBM 2006 Global CEO Study*, we found that 65 per cent of leaders anticipate fundamental change in their industries within the next two years.[2] As a strategic response, many CEOs are innovating in operations and/ or products and services. But we found that the financial outperformers put twice as much emphasis on business model innovation as underperformers (see Figure 1). As one CEO said, "Products and services can be copied; the business model is the differentiator."[3]

> ...one factor that often separates the winners from the losers is an ability to transform, or even to scrap, old ways of doing things and introduce new business models.

So we asked the CEOs who were focused on business model innovation to describe how they were approaching it. The majority cited reorganization and strategic partnerships. This fits well with our understanding of the increasingly extended and geographically integrated nature of enterprises, with technology and other factors enabling broader collaboration among employees worldwide, as well as with suppliers, customers and other partners.

Beyond this broad definition, however, we all – the CEOs, the IBM CEO Study Team, academics and other analysts – felt the need to delve deeper and ask: What do we mean exactly by business model innovation and, more importantly, what really matters in terms of financial performance? What, overall, are some guidelines for CEOs to follow as they navigate the new competitive landscape?

Building on the work of Fernand Braudel, Carlota Perez, Alvin Toffler and others, we can identify patterns in the seeming chaos of economic transformations.[4] While the specifics of the theories vary, there is a general understanding that what starts as scientific discovery soon generates commercially viable innovation. These innovations then generate an early round of new businesses and new business models that transform the economy.

Eventually, as the adoption of these innovations matures and as opportunities to leverage these innovations in older industries are realized, broader changes in the structure of businesses and in society – at the local, national and global levels – occur. When this happens, there are winners and losers and, often, painful periods of adjustment.[5]

For business leaders, failure to navigate these periods can lead to corporate decline or even extinction. Comparing the S&P 500 from 1957 with 2007, we found that even major players fell down the list or simply disappeared, as happened to Pan Am and Bethlehem Steel. In fact, only 16 per cent of the companies listed on the S&P 500 in 1957 remain there today.[6]

While post-mortems indicate a variety of causes for corporate decline or failure, one factor that often separates the winners from the losers is an ability to transform, or even to scrap, old ways of doing things and introduce new business models. This may at times require cannibalizing existing lines of business within an organization.[7] It may also mean moving into new industries, often by leveraging core capabilities while changing offerings.[8] Or it may mean having to manage diverse business models within one organization. For new firms with no legacies to defend and green fields to explore, the opportunities can be vast. In all cases, a vision of what is possible – not what was – must prevail.

Navigating such change using business model innovation is easier said than done in real time, however. And CEOs today clearly understand the magnitude of the challenges they face. Is there a roadmap, we asked, that might guide business leaders along the often treacherous path to successful business model innovation?

A framework for business model innovation

When we looked more deeply into the topic of business models and business model innovation, we found that, as with art, business leaders may know it when they see it, but they have difficulty defining it. Searching the literature on the topic proved similarly fruitless, providing no clear or generally accepted definition of business models or business model innovation. Many different views exist, each emphasizing different dimensions.

To help remedy this, based on our experience, an extensive literature review and an analysis of our 35 best practice cases, plus a scan of more than a dozen others, we developed a framework for understanding business model innovation and identified three main types of strategy.

The three types of business model innovation strategies are:

- **Industry model:** This approach involves innovating the "industry value chain." This can be accomplished via horizontal moves into new industries, as Virgin has done with its moves from music and retail into such diverse industries as airlines, railways, beverages, financial services and more, thus leveraging its superior skills in consumer management.

  It can also be accomplished by redefining existing industries, as Dell has done by eliminating intermediaries and going directly to customers and as Apple has done by delivering music directly to customers via iTunes.

  Perhaps most dramatically, industry model innovation can also involve the development of entirely new industries or industry segments, as Google and other search engine companies have done in the past decade. This dimension leverages white spaces in the competitive environment as well as unique assets.

- **Revenue model:** This approach involves innovations in how companies generate revenues by reconfiguring offerings (product/service/value mix) and/or by introducing new pricing models. This is a dimension that leverages customer experience, choices and preferences and one that can also leverage new technologies.

  A good example of an offering innovation is Cirque du Soleil's redefinition of the circus experience, combining new and old elements to change the value proposition and reach a new target audience.

  A classic example of a pricing innovation is Gillette's strategy of underpricing razors to sell razor blades. A more recent example is Netflix's introduction of a new kind of movie rental option, offering monthly subscriptions rather than the familiar product-based rental structure. New pricing models can also be seen in digitized modern markets with such offerings as music subscriptions and downloaded ring tones.

- **Enterprise model:** This approach involves innovating the structure of the enterprise and the role it plays in new or existing value chains. This dimension focuses on redefining organizational boundaries. Innovations here can be achieved through integration – as in the Japanese keiretsu framework, where what might

> A good example of an offering innovation is Cirque du Soleil's redefinition of the circus experience ...
>
> A classic example of a pricing innovation is Gillette's strategy of underpricing razors to sell razor blades

typically be a supply chain is owned and managed by one firm or conglomerate. Clothing retailer Zara, for example, manages design through delivery, creating feedback loops from customer data at stores to all parts of the organizational chain.[9] Enterprise model innovation can also be accomplished via specialization, wherein organizations focus on core competencies or high-margin activities and outsource the rest. The Indian telecommunications company Bharti Airtel, for example, focuses on marketing, sales and distribution, outsourcing much of the actual IT and networking functions to external partners.[10] Finally, enterprise model innovation can be accomplished via network plays, wherein companies rely on external collaboration. For example, illycaffé has partnered with various other companies along its value chain, such as manufacturers of coffee-makers and others, to improve the overall coffee-drinking experience.[11]

FIGURE 2. Breakdown of the 35 best practice cases used in our business model innovation analysis.

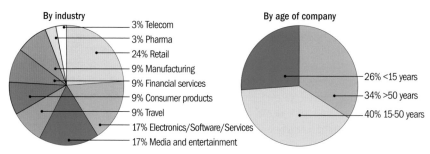

Source: IBM Institute for Business Value.

Using this three-dimensional framework to describe diverse but often complementary types of business model innovation, we then conducted a detailed analysis of 35 best practice cases using publicly available information. Fifteen of these cases were from the *BusinessWeek* 2006 list of leading business model innovators, including Apple, IKEA, Southwest Airlines and others.[12] We selected the remaining 20 cases based on a company's reputation for leadership in business model innovation as reflected in analyst reports, interviews with experts in diverse industries and a broad literature review.[13] The cases represent diverse industries, regions and types of business model innovation (see Figure 2).

For each of the 35 best practice cases, we assigned values of high, medium or low along three dimensions, indicating the type and extent of business model innovations used. Where companies had tried a variety of business model innovations through the years, we selected one particularly innovative, widely recognized and/or effective example. We then correlated business model innovation with various factors, including industry, period of innovation, age of company and size of company by number of employees, revenues and assets. This framework can be used as a diagnostic tool for identifying and evaluating business model innovation options. Finally, we conducted extensive financial analyses for 24 publicly traded companies in our sample. We used operating profit margin compound annual growth rate (CAGR) from 2001-2006 and stock price CAGR from 1996-2006 (or, in cases where the IPO was later than 1996, from the IPO to 2006). We then correlated financial performance with business model innovation, testing for various factors that might influence success.

As noted previously, we found from the IBM 2006 Global CEO Study that financial outperformers were putting twice as much emphasis on business model innovation as underperformers. But what exactly, we wanted to know, were top performers doing to innovate their business models and which approaches were most effective?[14]

All three paths can lead to success ...

Based on our analyses (see Figure 3), we found that all three types (or combinations) of business model innovation can lead to financial success. We found no significant variation in financial performance across the different types of business model innovation. The good news: With a sound overarching business strategy and strong execution, any of the paths can lead to success.

Much can be learned from entrepreneurs, or those companies in our study with less than 15 years in operation, who often lead the way when it comes to business model innovation. In particular, new entrants such as Google demonstrate the financial rewards to be gained by exploiting new technologies in original ways, in the process introducing extremely disruptive business model innovations.

FIGURE 3. **10-year stock CAGR versus type of business model innovation.**

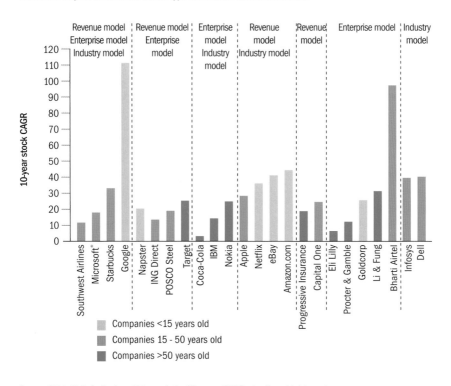

Source: IBM Institute for Business Value analysis of Thomson ONE Banker financial data and company annual reports, 1997-2006.

While breakthrough, headline-grabbing innovations are often initiated by new entrants, opportunities for revolutionary change exist for firms at virtually any stage. Nokia, for example, has evolved since its founding in 1865 as a paper mill company, repeatedly reinventing itself and the industries it has entered.[15]

Within industries, we find again that many paths can lead to success. Diverse strategies, when aligned with a company's brand, operations, core strengths, and other assets, can work for different companies in the same industry. For example, in financial services, an industry undergoing massive consolidation, Capital One and ING Direct have both been successful using different types of business model innovation.

Where Capital One has developed extensive customer data analysis, customer segmentation and micro-marketing strategies (revenue model innovation), ING Direct has exploited the Internet to lower its operating costs, offer higher interest rates and attract more consumers to online banking – in close cooperation with other financial institutions (enterprise model innovation).[16]

... but network plays are key

While many paths may lead to successful business model innovation, innovations in enterprise structure that focus on network plays or external collaboration proved to be the most common type of business model innovation in our sample. In fact, almost half of the cases we studied focused extensively on this strategy.

Companies using these strategies had equally strong financial results as those using other types of business model innovation. For example, as noted above, Indian telecommunications maverick Bharti Airtel has developed an organizational structure that is centered heavily on its extended network, enabling it to radically lower prices and expand its customer base while specializing in customer relationships, not technology.[17]

Among the older companies in our sample, enterprise or network plays were particularly common, enabling them to change course via new partnerships or acquisitions while leveraging their brand, scale, channels or other long-standing strengths. For example, illycaffé has partnered extensively with companies that produce coffee cups and coffee makers in order to enhance the overall experience for its customers, as mentioned previously. In another example, Eli Lilly has established a "research without walls" strategy of partnering with biotech companies, academic institutions and others to strengthen their innovation pipeline.[18] In these and other cases, relying solely on internal R&D would probably have been more expensive and slower.

This is not to say, however, that such collaboration is easy to implement and manage. In the *2006 Global CEO Study*, 76 per cent of CEOs cited the importance of enabling collaborative innovation, yet only 51 per cent reported that they were actually doing this to a large extent.[19]

One big challenge is that, as organizations become more global, they face more complex issues related to culture, regulation, technology and other areas. Furthermore, with the growing trend toward extended enterprise models, which involve more external partnerships, collaborative innovation is even harder to do well.

Multiple sources show that failure rates for strategic partnerships exceed 50 per cent, with problems related to collaboration across organizations thought to be a key cause.[20] The fact that the best practice cases we analyzed have succeeded in external collaboration shows that those innovation leaders who are able to overcome the gap between idea and execution find a powerful way to differentiate themselves.

PINPOINTING YOUR STRENGTHS, SHORTCOMINGS AND OPTIONS FOR BUSINESS MODEL INNOVATION

Understanding ways to leverage business model innovation is a key source of competitive advantage in today's economy. The following questions can help you assess your options and develop a roadmap to effective business model innovation:

Understanding the industry context

- What new business models do you see emerging in your industry? Is the basis for competition changing?
- Where are new and disruptive business models coming from – within your industry or from new players/other industries?
- What is the degree of change and innovation in your industry? What can you learn from successful business model innovators – either in your industry or outside?

Defining your position

- How does your degree of innovation relate to your industry? Do you have the balance right between incremental versus more radical innovations?
- Do you drive the change in your industry, or is it imposed on you? Are disruptive models emerging in areas you are not focusing on today?
- Which business model innovation paths are you exploring? Which models are most aligned with your industry, capability and vision?

Building your capabilities to manage business model innovation

- Industry models: Do you have a systematic way to envision future industry scenarios and implications for your innovation strategy?
- Revenue models: How can you exploit new/emerging revenue models as well as new value offerings, and manage the implications for your business and competitive positioning? Do you have a structured approach to thinking through revenue implications?
- Enterprise models: Do you understand – and leverage – your unique capabilities and assets? What capabilities and processes do you have in place to develop, maintain, evaluate and terminate external collaboration for innovation?

Conclusion

Anticipating massive change across diverse industries, top-performing CEOs are focusing on business model innovation as a path to competitive power and growth. To accomplish this, business leaders can utilize three main types of business model innovation: innovation in industry models, revenue models and/or enterprise models. These approaches to business model innovation can be used alone or in combination.

The good news is that with the right strategy and strong execution, all paths can lead to successful business model innovation. At the same time, however, enterprise model innovation, emphasizing collaboration and partnerships, is the most common strategy. And the companies we studied that are pursuing enterprise model innovation focusing on collaboration and partnerships achieved financial results comparable to those using other business model innovation strategies.

About the authors

Edward Giesen is the Leader in Europe, the Middle East and Africa for Business Strategy and Component Business Modeling within the Strategy and Change practice for IBM Global Business Services. He can be reached at edward.giesen@nl.ibm.com.

Saul Berman is the Services Leader for the Strategy and Change practice of IBM Global Business Services. He is also the Global and Americas Media and Entertainment Strategy and Change Lead Partner. He can be reached at saul.berman@us.ibm.com.

Ragna Bell is the Global Business Solutions Portfolio Manager within Strategy and Change for IBM Global Business Services. She can be reached at ragna.bell@us.ibm.com.

Amy Blitz is the Strategy and Change Lead for the Institute for Business Value within IBM Global Business Services. She can be contacted at ablitz@us.ibm.com.

Contributors

The authors are indebted to many throughout IBM for their substantial contributions to this paper. We thank first Mahesh

Ganesan for his extensive role in developing the literature review and the detailed case analyses. We also thank Jamie Bader, Chris Benne, Rob Berini, Alain Biem, Marc Chapman, Michael Gibney, Stephen Hines, Jeff Hittner, Peter Korsten, Daniel Latimore, Dave Lubowe, Lawrence Owen, George Pohle, Stephen Reiser, and Robert Scavello for their insights and contributions. In the spirit of collaboration and partnering, we thank these colleagues and many others in the extended IBM team who have contributed to this paper.

References

1 "Expanding the Innovation Horizon: The Global CEO Study 2006." IBM Global Business Services. March 2006. http://www.ibm.com/bcs/ceostudy. In this study, IBM interviewed 765 CEOs, business executives and public sector leaders worldwide to understand the innovation challenges faced by companies globally.

2 Ibid.

3 Ibid.

4 Main works by Braudel, Perez and Toffler include: Braudel, Fernand, *Civilization and Capitalism, 15th-18th Century,* Berkeley: University of California Press, 1992; Perez, Carlota, *Technological Revolutions and Financial Capital: The Dynamics of Bubbles and Golden Ages,* Cheltenham, UK and Northampton, MA: E. Elgar Publishers, 2002; and Toffler, Alvin, *The Third Wave,* New York: Morrow Publishers, 1980.

5 For example, the development of the steam engine at the end of the 18th century soon led to new business opportunities in transportation and manufacturing, which, in turn, led to new ways of producing goods such as cotton. As new business models disrupted earlier ones, some businesses and the social structures surrounding them died while others replaced them. The U.S. Civil War is one example of the kind of painful adjustment that can accompany such economic change.

6 IBM Institute for Business Value analysis, using data from the Standard & Poors archives for 1957 and from the Standard & Poors website for 2007. The original 1957 list is available at http://www2.standardandpoors.com/spf/pdf/index/030207_86Survivors-Release.pdf

7 Christensen, Clayton M. *The Innovator's Dilemma: When New Technologies Cause Great Firms to Fail.* Boston, Massachusetts: Harvard Business School Press. 1997.

8 de Geus, Andre. *The Living Company.* Boston, Massachusetts: Harvard Business School Press. April 1997.

9 Helft, Miguel. "Fashion Fast Forward." *Business 2.0.* May 2002.

10 de Asis Martinez-Jerez, F., V. G. Narayanan and Michele Jurgens. "Strategic Outsourcing at Bharti Airtel Ltd." Harvard Business School Publishing. July 12, 2006.

11 "Francis Francis! Espresso Machines Offer Beauty and Superiority for Seamless Coffee Preparation." illycaffé press release, June 27, 2006. http://www.illy.com/usa/about_illy/press_room/press_releases/Francis_Francis_Espresso_Machines.htm

12 "The World's Most Innovative Companies." *BusinessWeek.* April 24, 2006. http://www.businessweek.com/magazine/content/06_17/b3981401.htm

13 The remaining 20 companies selected for analysis included Adsoncars, Bharti Airtel, Capital One, Chongqing Motorcyles, Cirque du Soleil, Coca-Cola, Eli Lilly, Flexcar, Gillette, GoldCorp, Infosys, illycaffé, ING Direct, Li & Fung, Netflix, the new Napster, POSCO Steel, Progressive Insurance, Zara and a major entertainment company.

14 "Expanding the Innovation Horizon: The Global CEO Study 2006." IBM Global Business Services. March 2006. http://www.ibm.com/bcs/ceostudy

15 "Story of Nokia." http://www.nokia.com/A4303001

16 For information on Capital One's micro-marketing strategies, see: Zack, Michael H."Rethinking the Knowledge-Based Organization." *Sloan Management Review.* Vol. 44, No. 4, Summer 2003, pp. 67-71. For information on ING Direct's approach, see: "ING takes low-cost route to expansion." *The Banker.* September 3, 2003.

17 de Asis Martinez-Jerez, F., V. G. Narayanan and Michele Jurgens. "Strategic Outsourcing at Bharti Airtel Ltd." Harvard Business School Publishing. July 12, 2006.

18 "Achieving value through partnership." Eli Lilly and Company. http://www.lilly.com/about/partnering/alliances/index.html

19 "Expanding the Innovation Horizon: The Global CEO Study 2006." IBM Global Business Services. March 2006. http://www.ibm.com/bcs/ceostudy

20 Ernst, David and James Bamford. "Your Alliances Are Too Stable." *Harvard Business Review.* June 2005.

"You have to go down blind alleys. But every once in a while you go down an alley and it opens up into this huge, broad avenue. That makes all the blind alleys worthwhile."

Jeffrey P. Bezos, Chairman, President and CEO, Amazon.com Inc.

Hof, Robert D. "Building An Idea Factory." BusinessWeek Online. October 11, 2004.
http://www.businessweek.com/magazine/content/04_41/b3903462.htm

Speaking of innovation 2

CHRIS ROBERTS is the president and CEO of Cochlear Limited, the world leader in hearing implant technology. Based in Sydney, Australia, Cochlear holds about 70 per cent of the global implant market and its revenues have grown by about 20 per cent a year for the past decade. Cochlear generates most of its income from Europe and the Americas, but sees the Asia-Pacific region, and China in particular, as fundamental to the company's future. Dr. Roberts is also the chairman of Research Australia, a not-for-profit organization that promotes Australian health and medical research.

Q: Where are Cochlear's innovative energies focused?
A: We've had exponential growth for 25 years and still there's a huge unmet clinical need. More people are born deaf or go deaf every year – and meet our criteria for an implant – than receive an implant. So our market is growing. This is the 25th anniversary of one of our implants being put in a patient and over those years our innovation has absolutely been focused on technological innovation. That's my background – the understanding that technological innovation is the turbocharger for growth for a company or indeed a country. Even 25 years down the track we're still spending 12 per cent of revenues on R&D. But looking at where this business is today, we have to innovate our business model in addition to product innovation. At one end that's about our consumer health-care activities – for example, consumer advocacy activities to drive patients with hearing loss to receive appropriate health services. At the other end, it's about being a world-class service delivery company. It's about coming up with better ways of supporting patients after they receive our implant. That's a fundamentally different way of thinking about the business, as opposed to being just a medical device company that makes something, sells it to a doctor or hospital, and then they have to worry about trying to find the patients and look after them later on.

But it's very challenging. With R&D at least you have a group of people focused on delivering that. But it's hard to change your business model across Europe, where you might have 26 languages and five alphabets. And the way business is done in those countries is really very different, so it's hard to get scale and leverage across that. It's a lot easier in the US, for example, which tends to be more homogeneous. So while there are all these great activities being done at a local level in Europe, the question is how do we get scale and leverage across Europe? And across the Asia-Pacific. So innovating the business model has presented us with significantly different obstacles to technological innovation.

Q: How hard is it to get people thinking about the future and the opportunities it holds?
A: People struggle with designing what the future ought to look like. It's about four things for me: the competencies we want; how much of those we want, or the capacity of those competencies; scale; and leverage. It's about getting those four things across our global operations. So if someone's repairing 50 of something a week, what resources will they need when they're doing 100 a week? Or if they're doing 1000 invoices a day, what will they need when they're doing 2000 invoices a day? And I find people really struggle with that. I guess that came out of problems with developing two- and three-year plans, which tend to be spreadsheet exercises in which the second and third years are just mathematical increments on the first year. It's a complete and utter waste of time. It's not insightful. So I've tried to create a dialogue around what the next doubling of the business looks like. I find that's easier. Don't worry about how long it takes you to double, but if you're doing twice as many of something, what's that going to look like?

That's still difficult because, outside engineering, people get very little exposure to design. Accountancy or law or finance or science or marketing – none of these things teaches you anything about design, whereas there are a lot of basic tools in engineering that help when it comes to designing the future. So it's no wonder that most people struggle with things like innovating the business model. Which means you've got to help people think about what can be different and how we can make it different. You have to create opportunities for people to be creative, to look at things with different angles. And, of course, you have to create enough thinking time for people.

However, you should also recognize that a lot of people in the organization are really just about delivering today's stuff.

Q: How do you approach collaboration outside the organization?
A: We are working with probably 60 institutions around the world, typically universities. And we've just announced that we are relocating to the campus of Macquarie University, which is one of the big three universities in Sydney. We want to get links going right through our organization into that university. And that's what the university wants as well. And this is not just about technological innovation. It's about thinking in HR and all sorts of areas of the business. Also, Macquarie University has a world-class audiology department and they're doing interesting things in linguistics. So together we're looking at developing a hearing precinct, in which a lot of other activities around hearing can be brought onto campus. It's in the university's interests and in our interests to have maybe 2000 people working in the area of hearing. This is an opportunity to create different inputs and linkages that aren't easy to create otherwise. That's hugely innovative, I think. You might say, "Why can't you do it now? They're only six miles up the road." But the reality is that six miles can be a long way compared with being on campus.

"Everyone should be dissatisfied with the present situation…That's what needs to be recognized by every individual. When you're growing, you're satisfied with the status quo, and that's no good."

Katsuaki Watanabe, President, Toyota

Green, William and Michiko Tomoya. "Toyota's Tough Boss." Time. September 18, 2005. http://www.time.com/time/globalbusiness/article/0,9171,1106335,00.html

The power of many

ABCs of collaborative innovation

Lawrence Owen, Charles Goldwasser,
Kristi Choate and Amy Blitz

To drive innovation, many top CEOs are collaborating beyond their organizations – with their extended networks of suppliers, customers, business partners and others. Such collaboration, however, is easier said than done. In fact, an estimated 50 per cent of strategic alliances fail. Based on our research, experience and two best practice cases, we have developed a framework – the ABCs of collaborative innovation – that can improve the chances of success in this increasingly important area.

Expanding the Innovation Horizon found that CEOs place a high priority on innovation in response to shifts in the global marketplace. While companies were pursuing the three main types of innovation – in products, services and markets; in operations; and in business models – the study found that financial outperformers were putting twice as much emphasis on business model innovation as underperformers. Further, in describing business model innovation, CEOs focused on organizational issues, notably changes in organizational structure and more extensive external strategic partnerships.

This emphasis indicates that CEOs are increasingly looking beyond their internal R&D teams for ideas and innovation. In fact, study results showed that only 17 per cent of the CEOs were relying on R&D for innovative ideas. The most common sources were employees (41 per cent), followed by business partners (38 per cent) and customers (37 per cent). Clearly, as innovation expands throughout the organization and beyond, the need to enable collaboration for innovation becomes increasingly important. Indeed, the strongest financial performers in our study were also the strongest collaborators.

There is a gap, however, between the ideal and the reality. While 76 per cent of CEOs cited the importance of enabling collaborative innovation, only 51 per cent reported that they were actually doing this to a large extent. One big challenge is that, as organizations become more global, they face more complex issues related to culture, regulation, technology and other areas. Further, with the growing trend toward extended enterprise models, involving more external partnerships, collaborative innovation is even harder to do well. Research shows that failure rates for strategic alliances hover near 50 per cent.[1]

A framework for collaboration

To avoid the pitfalls of collaborative innovation, our research and experience show the best building blocks are: alignment, boundaries and commitment. Alignment entails synchronizing the strategic vision and innovation goals with the implementation of these throughout the organization, focusing on collaboration both vertically and horizontally. Managing boundaries enables collaboration across organizations, establishing structures and processes regarding governance, operations and technology. Finally, sustained commitment is required to orchestrate and systematize collaboration for innovation throughout the organization and its extended enterprise. These ABCs can be done separately or in combination, depending on the capabilities, strategic goals and innovation objectives of the organization. Note that by calling these the "ABCs" we do not mean to imply that this is in any way easy, but rather that there is a way of simplifying the complexities of collaborative innovation (see Figure 1).

FIGURE 1. **The ABCs of successful collaboration.**

Alignment
The strategy and organization must be aligned vertically and horizontally to support the collaboration for innovation agenda.

Boundaries
Strategic relationships with the extended enterprise must be defined and managed for optimal collaboration.

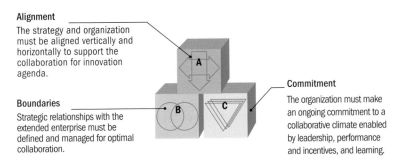

Commitment
The organization must make an ongoing commitment to a collaborative climate enabled by leadership, performance and incentives, and learning.

Source: IBM Institute for Business Value.

A = Alignment

Alignment is a key step in ensuring that the business strategy is communicated and enabled throughout the organization vertically and horizontally. Alignment requires looking at the organization from the perspective of innovation objectives, and then using the insights gained to position the organization to meet those objectives.

Vertical alignment translates the business strategy's innovation objectives into an organizational strategy and an implementation plan. Once translated, the business strategy provides a roadmap for change.

Horizontal alignment typically requires the creation of a new organizational unit or the redefinition of existing ones. Key here is the elimination of structures and processes that may have been effective in the past but are no longer conducive to collaborative innovation. In the process, horizontal alignment reduces barriers to collaboration across functional groups, divisions, geographies and other "silos". To make collaboration for innovation systemic, there also needs to be a focus on how people will actually get work done. Often, job functions, responsibilities and performance measurements will need to be altered to include collaboration for innovation. Changes in HR approaches (such as recruitment, selection, compensation and training) further ingrain collaboration for innovation into the culture.

By translating the business strategy into operational goals, and by creating structures and processes to enable collaboration across all segments of the organization, innovation leaders can motivate and enable new behavior.

B = Boundaries

As noted previously, the majority of strategic partnerships fail, and they typically do so because they are very hard to manage well. They require building trust, navigating different approaches to decision-making, agreeing to legal terms about ownership and other often contentious issues, collaborating across cultures, managing communications and operations, and so on.

To avoid these problems, identifying the best partner is the first critical step. Potential partners may include customers, suppliers, government groups or others. Establishing the right structure, such as a joint venture, strategic alliance or consortium, is essential and must extend from the company's innovation agenda and business strategy. Here, it is important to understand the history and culture of each group as well as the goals and terms of the relationship. Will the relationship be temporary or permanent, physical or virtual, rigid or flexible? Are any legal agreements needed to protect specific interests? As these and other questions are explored, governance needs to be established, covering potential areas of conflict such as ownership of intellectual property and decision-making processes. The financial and contractual agreements that result from these discussions are crucial to the success of the relationship.

Technological integration and data visibility across organizations are also critical factors, enabling partners to communicate and share information.

Strong collaborative tools are increasingly important. IBM, for example, uses what it calls "Innovation Jams," Web-based applications that allow multiple users from inside the company and from several other participating organizations to have threaded discussions on diverse topics. In establishing the technological foundations, various requirements and protocols must be evaluated, understood and established. For example, will interactions be physical or virtual, or both? Addressed early and fully, technology can greatly advance collaborative innovation.

In all cases, defining the partnership, establishing governance terms and then building a technological and operational infrastructure for collaboration across organizations can significantly improve the chances of success. When the boundaries are managed well, collaborative innovation can occur among external partners and internal stakeholders (see Figure 2).

FIGURE 2. Optimal relationships depend on well-defined boundaries throughout the extended enterprise.

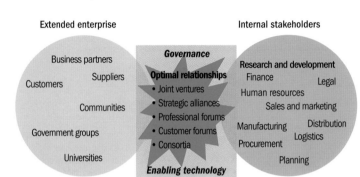

Source: IBM Institute for Business Value.

C = Commitment

Organizations that are serious about collaboration for innovation make a sustained commitment to transformation and change. Creating a collaborative culture happens over time through leadership communication and reinforcement, the development and tracking of key measures, and institutionalized learning and knowledge management to develop the capabilities needed for collaborative innovation (see Figure 3).

Of the collaboration ABCs, aligning the organization and establishing boundaries with partners often have identifiable start and end points. The third component, however, represents persistent work to infuse the organizational culture and to drive leadership's commitment to the broad goal of enabling and rewarding collaborative innovation.

Three elements make up the commitment component of the framework: leadership; performance management; and learning and improving.

- Leadership is needed to develop and communicate the strategic direction of collaborative innovation throughout the organization. Leaders define and work toward attaining the cultural attributes that are needed for better collaboration (such as open versus closed and risk-taking versus risk-averse). They commit to establishing an organizational climate that fosters internal and external collaboration. They also must eliminate organizational elements that act as barriers to collaboration.
- Performance management adds structure to the leadership vision.

FIGURE 3. Commitment involves sustained efforts to mature
the organization's abilities to collaborate for innovation.

Leadership
Leadership shows sustained commitment with a focus on collaborative climate,
removal of barriers and strategic marketing of the innovation agenda.

Learning
The organization defines and builds
needed capabilities based on a
philosophy of learning and improving the
collaboration approach.

Performance and incentives
Owning outcomes and recognizing
desired behaviors and results
reinforces collaboration.

Source: IBM Institute for Business Value.

By outlining a standard approach to assess, select, contract, operate, evaluate and end collaborative partnerships, the handling of such relationships becomes more consistent. To be able to motivate and reward collaboration, it is vital to establish performance measurements and reward approaches.

- Continuous learning and improvement are also critical. This includes defining and building capabilities for idea generation, relationship management and collaboration. For optimal results, knowledge gained through collaboration should be captured, shared and reused. The goal here is to improve collaborative innovation over time by establishing processes for learning and change.

Putting the ABCs into play

Eli Lilly and Company launches "research without walls": Eli Lilly and Company is a strong example of a company that helped set the standards in its industry for collaborative innovation. The pharmaceutical industry faces continual pressure to launch more innovative products as quickly and cost-effectively as possible. To address these needs, pharmaceutical companies rely increasingly on external sources of innovation as a way to accelerate, strengthen and deepen their innovation pipelines.

In the mid-1990s, Lilly's senior management recognized a growing

---

SNAPSHOT: THE ABCs AT ELI LILLY

Alignment:

A "research without walls" strategy driven by leadership was designed to revitalize the new product development pipeline. Alignment across all functions of the organization enabled greater collaboration among R&D, business development, sales and marketing, legal and other functions. The Sourcing Innovation Group, in particular, brought R&D prospecting, corporate business development and a newly created Office of Alliance Management together under one structure, helping ensure these groups were aligned.

Boundaries:

Through the Office of Alliance Management, boundaries with external partners, including biotechnology firms and academic institutions, are carefully negotiated and managed to address governance, ownership, risk, IP and other issues. Regular surveys of partners are also administered and studied to test the health of the relationships.

Commitment:

Lilly's Office of Alliance Management and the broader Sourcing Innovation group have been particularly effective in optimizing the company's relationships with external partners. In addition, new organizations, such as InnoCentive, have been established to enable collaborative innovation in areas related to drug discovery.

---

need to strengthen its innovation pipeline and better position itself to discover, develop and ultimately launch new medicines at the start of the next decade. To meet this need, Lilly developed a creative solution. Using what it called a "research without walls" approach, Lilly began to cultivate an extensive network of external partners in biotech, academia and other innovation centers as a major component of its overall innovation strategy.

The company's early adoption of the "research without walls" approach would prove valuable as Lilly entered the new millennium. In 2001, Lilly's largest-selling product, the anti-depressant Prozac, lost patent protection earlier than expected, resulting in a sizable loss of revenue. At the same time, the company was experiencing delays in U.S. Food and Drug Administration approval to launch several new drugs in its pipeline, and a recently launched sepsis drug was not as successful as anticipated.

> Lilly has been benchmarked as best in-class for managing alliances, an increasingly critical success factor in the pharmaceutical industry.

To jumpstart and better focus its external collaboration efforts, Lilly made the decision in 2001 to bring its R&D prospecting group, its corporate business development group and a newly created Office of Alliance Management together under one organization known as "Sourcing Innovation." By bringing these areas together, Lilly helped break down barriers among groups that might otherwise have competed. In the process, Lilly also facilitated a broader commitment to collaboration. Moreover, by creating an Office of Alliance Management, Lilly ensured a systematic approach to its growing network of external partners.

Today the Office of Alliance Management handles more than 100 R&D partnerships focused on new technology, products and services, while others in manufacturing work with an additional 160 partnerships. Using surveys of partners, the office regularly tests the health of each relationship and identifies areas for improvement. The group also creates roadmaps for designing, negotiating and managing alliances to ensure sustainability and value to all parties. Moreover, the office studies and implements findings from its numerous alliances in order to avoid the myriad organizational, governance, technological and other issues that can derail even the most promising partnerships.

> "Successful alliances are more critical than ever to our strategy. We are working hard to be recognized as the pharmaceutical industry's premier partner by consistently creating value for our partners and for Lilly."
>
> *Sidney Taurel, Chairman of the Board and Chief Executive Officer, Eli Lilly and Company* [2]

In addition to these efforts, Lilly created a novel business model for collaborative innovation when it started InnoCentive. This company, which Lilly has subsequently spun off but still retains some ownership of, leverages the global reach of the internet to bring together "seeker" companies with "solver" scientists to identify innovative solutions to diverse problems. To date, InnoCentive has registered more than 110,000 "solvers" in more than 175 countries. [3]

The results of Lilly's "research without walls" efforts have been impressive. The company has launched numerous new products, invigorated its innovation pipeline and achieved revenue growth as well as solid branding as a partner of choice. A sampling of partnerships – and the revenues they generated in 2006 alone – demonstrates the link from collaboration to innovation to financial performance. For example, Byetta, developed by Amylin Pharmaceuticals and now manufactured and co-marketed by Lilly, was launched in June 2005 and generated revenue for 2006 of $US430 million. Other successes for 2006 include Cialis, which generated $US971 million, and Actos, which generated $US448 million. Lilly is now working with another partner, Daiichi Sankyo, toward FDA submission of Prasugrel, a promising anti-clotting compound.

Lilly has been benchmarked as best-in-class for managing alliances, an increasingly critical success factor in the pharmaceutical industry.

Airbus collaborates for innovative lift: In the tightly competitive aerospace industry, Airbus has found a way to accelerate innovation: by working closely with its extensive network of suppliers and other partners to develop innovative solutions collaboratively.[4]

An aerospace industry leader in developing new technologies, Airbus has faced serious pressures in getting its new A380, the world's largest passenger plane, to market. Amid many challenges, an area of success has been in the wing assembly, one of the most complex parts of the aircraft. Based in the United Kingdom, the wing assembly group collaborated closely with an extended network of suppliers to identify innovative solutions to complex issues, and in the process to cut production time and meet schedule commitments.

The first step was a shift from being a development organization to one that manages large-scale serial production. As part of this shift, the Airbus UK wing division had to coordinate the efforts of its extended network of suppliers, sub-contractors and others. An experienced team of human resource and organizational specialists

---

SNAPSHOT: THE ABCs AT AIRBUS

Alignment:
The company's business goals for A380 production were vertically aligned throughout the organization. Management layers were removed to enable UK country team leaders to make key decisions, greatly accelerating the pace of collaboration with suppliers.

Boundaries:
Through careful negotiations with many suppliers involved in the wing production, Airbus resolved challenging issues related to ownership, risk-sharing, governance and IP. Extensive training initiatives then enabled standardization throughout the diverse group of supplier organizations.

Commitment:
Airbus established internal teams to manage key supplier relationships and establish clear, consistent collaboration for innovation across organizations.

---

was brought in to help, delivering specialized training programs for several hundred people across Airbus UK and its many subcontractors in new tools, processes and collaborative approaches.

These and other initiatives greatly accelerated wing production, with overall lead time reduced by 41 weeks, or 36 per cent. In addition, Airbus achieved significant cost improvements in design and manufacturing. Overall, collaboration with suppliers, subcontractors and others helped identify innovation solutions throughout wing development for the A380. And though the company continues to struggle with timelines for getting the A380 to market, in this area, it soared.

Pinpointing your strengths and shortfalls

To begin an analysis of your own company's collaboration capabilities, ask yourself the following questions based on the ABC framework.

Alignment

- To what extent is your overall business strategy supported by a strategy for collaborative innovation?
- How well do people at all levels of the organization understand the overall strategic direction and associated innovation goals? How strongly do they identify with these? Do they know how their actions contribute?
- Are the right processes in place to drive or support innovation at all levels of the organization, in operations, in business models and in the development of new offerings? In manufacturing, sales, corporate development?
- How well connected are the components of your organization to support innovation, including R&D and sales?

Boundaries

- How well does your business model, operations and product portfolio support collaboration with partners outside your company?
- How visible are these partnerships throughout your organization? How structured are the processes for collaborating with external partners? Are roles and responsibilities for managing collaboration understood internally and externally?
- In what ways are your processes, governance and operating guidelines

designed specifically to facilitate sharing information with other companies? Do you have structures for resolving or avoiding conflicts over IP, ownership and other core issues?

- How does your technological infrastructure support collaborative processes across the extended enterprise, from basic communications to shared access to information to real-time collaboration?
- What kind of process do you have in place for monitoring and understanding potential changes in strategy or direction by any of your current and potential partners?

Commitment

- How strongly does your company culture value spending time, energy and resources on commercializing ideas obtained from outside?
- To what extent do leaders provide support for the strategic innovation agenda? How consistent is this over time?
- In what ways do your HR processes (hiring, training, performance management, incentives), reporting relationships, and other organizational structures support collaborative innovation?
- Does your collaboration strategy enable the agility necessary to accommodate dynamic partnering relationships?
- Does your organization capture lessons learned and apply these to future collaborations and, if so, to what degree?

  Based on your responses to these questions, are you comfortable that you are positioned to collaborate for innovation? If not, which areas do you plan to improve? Finally, do you have a balance between short-term interventions and long-term strategies for improving collaboration across your organization and extended enterprise?

Conclusion

Top CEOs recognize the need to make organizational changes to support collaborative innovation and derive profit from valuable ideas, no matter where they originate. The ABCs – alignment, boundaries and commitment – provide a framework for unlocking the power of many, enabling collaborative innovation throughout the extended enterprise and improving performance.

About the authors

Lawrence Owen is the Global Leader of the Organization and Change Strategy practice within IBM Global Business Services. He can be contacted at owenl@us.ibm.com.

Charles Goldwasser is the Americas Leader of the Organization and Change Strategy practice for IBM and the author of Action Management – Practical Strategies for Making Your Corporate Transformation a Success. *He can be reached at charlie.goldwasser@us.ibm.com.*

Kristi Choate is a Senior Managing Consultant in the IBM Organization and Change Strategy practice. She can be contacted at kristi.choate@us.ibm.com.

Amy Blitz is the Strategy and Change Leader for the IBM Institute for Business Value. Her work has been featured in Harvard Business Review, The New York Times, The Wall Street Journal, *MSNBC and PBS. She can be contacted at ablitz@us.ibm.com.*

Contributors

This paper would not have been possible without the insights and contributions of an extended IBM team, including Saul Berman, Susan Blum, Trevor Davis, Kathryn Everest, Ian Foraker, Andrew Gear, Chris Kirk, May Lawrence, Salima Manji Lin, Mike Martin, Philip Myburg, John Riley, Suzanne Simon, Andrew Statton and Andy Strowbridge.

References

[1] Ernst, David and James Bamford. "Your Alliances Are Too Stable." *Harvard Business Review.* June 2005.

[2] "Achieving value through partnership." Eli Lilly and Company. http://www.lilly.com/about/partnering/alliances/index.html

[3] "The Rockefeller Foundation to Extend InnoCentive's Online, Global Scientific Platform For Technology Solutions to Global Development Problems." InnoCentive press release. December 18, 2006.

[4] "Airbus achieves A380 first flight on schedule with help from IBM." IBM Corporation. January 2007. http://www-306.ibm.com/software/success/cssdb.nsf/cs/jsts-6wj2bz

"We will fight our battles not on the low road to commoditization, but on the high road of innovation."

Howard Stringer, Chairman and CEO, Sony

"Sony's Revitalization in the Changing CE World." Howard Stringer's remarks, CEATEC, Tokyo, October 4, 2005.
http://www.sony.com/SCA/speeches/051004_stringer.shtml

"All I've done since I got here is focus
on one word: innovation."

Ed Zander, Chairman and CEO, Motorola

"At Motorola, 'a Hop in Everybody's Step.'" BusinessWeek Online. August 22, 2005.
http://www.businessweek.com/magazine/content/05_32/b3946107_mz063.htm

Speaking of innovation 3

DOUGLAS MERRILL is a Vice-President of Engineering at Google. He joined Google late in 2003 as Senior Director of Information Systems. In that capacity he led multiple strategic efforts including Google's 2004 IPO and its related regulatory activities. He holds direct line accountability for all internal engineering and support worldwide.[1]

On building an environment that supports innovation
That's what I think we got right. We built a culture and a community of practice from the beginning that focuses on ensuring that we could keep the innovation engine going. Transformational innovations aren't enough. Our auction wasn't enough. You have to do a whole bunch of incremental innovations on top of that. And for any business to create value long-term they have to create additional transformational innovations. So we have a whole bunch of elements deeply embedded in our culture to ensure a climate of innovation.

Most importantly, we live out loud. We talk about everything. We'll talk about performance; we'll talk about technology. We have arguments all the time. Because we believe the best way to find a new idea is to get different people thinking about the same problem. We got our users to tell us what their problems were, by looking at the data or studying them etc., and then we got a bunch of very smart people who have different opinions to talk about them. So we try to hire people who have different backgrounds and different ways of thinking. And we put them in rooms together, and we pack them pretty tight in most offices, so that you get great innovative energy and lots of different perspectives. It's the reason we serve food. We don't serve food because we like having fat employees, although that's a perfectly fine side-effect (and we also provide gym membership). We provide food because, what do you do around the lunch table? What do you do around the dinner table? You talk, you engage, you interact. And we usually serve it at these big, long cafeteria-type tables so that you don't necessarily notice who you're sitting next to. We don't serve them at small tables where it's real easy to have a discussion with just your clique. So the person sitting next to you is going to weigh in on your input, on whatever it is that you happen to be talking about. Lots of input on the same problem. Lots of diverse perspectives living out loud drives innovation.

Experiment and learn from failure

Most innovations fail. Most evolutionary changes are irrelevant. You never notice them. Or they don't make any difference. My hair color is brown, not black. It makes no material difference to my life. Similarly, most innovations in business don't matter. Most are not actively destructive; they're just irrelevant. Those are failures. For cultures that punish you for failing, what will rapidly happen to the people who have ideas? They will rapidly stop sharing them. The hardest part of cultural change is actually to accept failure as part of the learning process and build support structures and processes around learning from failures. We've done that a lot. We experiment a lot and our value is in failing fast.

It's okay to run experiments as long as you follow it with data and do what the data says. I'll give you an example: our users used to tell us they wanted 20 search results on the main page instead of 10. Ten results takes about 400 milliseconds to respond. So we said, "Okay, fine." So we gave them 20 results. The top 10 results are the same; nothing material changes here. We just added 10 more. Nothing interesting happened, right? Instead of taking 400 milliseconds to respond, it took us 600 milliseconds. And we lost 15 per cent of our traffic. 'Cause they were bored waiting for the results. 200 milliseconds and they were bored! That's okay. We learned something: Speed matters.

Let people be passionate about what they're doing

One of the things that we do is what we call "20 per cent time". Our engineers are expected to spend 20 per cent of their time working on something that isn't their main project. Just something they're interested in. You can envisage this as being "Oh, every Friday I'm going to work on that." Engineers don't actually do that. They basically work for a couple of months on a project and then work a couple of weeks on a 20 per cent time project. Or they bank it up for a year and then do a month. Most of the time when I talk to other CIOs about this, what I get is: "Oh my God, that's incredibly stupid. That's such a huge tax on productivity. How can you possibly do that?" The answer is twofold. One: we get such a motivation boost out of it that the 80 per cent of time they're spending is way more productive than just 80 per cent of a normal engineer. And second: some of our very greatest projects have come out of 20 per cent time.

GoogleNews was a 20 per cent time project. Gmail was a 20 per cent product. The economic value created by these few of the 20 per cent projects more than pays for whatever the "tax" involved is.

On structure and chaos

Lots of companies want to structure their innovation – they have an innovation czar. They have an innovation process person. And when you have an idea you get to submit a business case and it includes a budget and then a committee of people will meet in a dark room smoking cigars and decide whether your innovation is worthy. We let there be chaos. Lots of 20 per cent time projects, lots of small projects starting up all the time – it creates total chaos. And then periodically we try to organise the chaos into themes, focus areas, strange attractors. And we try very hard not to kill the fragile little things. We measure success over time but we cull projects late. Rather than culling projects at start-up we have projects measure their per cent growth. Week over week, month over month, quarter over quarter, how many more users do you have as a per cent of what you had last time? If you're losing users, your project's not very good. If you're flat, you have an issue. If you're going up, you're interesting. And as you go up enough, we start investing in you and you go from a little tiny project to a much bigger project. We try to cull projects as late as we possibly can to give innovation – which is a very, very fragile flower – as long a spring as possible in which to thrive.

You have to be your own user

At Google we use our own products because that means we're more likely to see our users' problems more quickly and get more useful help. We recently migrated from a third-party calendar service to Google Calendar. It's a corporate version of the commercial program that lots of people in the world use today. We did it over a weekend and we moved about 600,000 events across. Users on the Internet filed bugs with us. They'd say things like: "Oh, Google Calendar didn't work to create this event last week." That's not a very helpful bug, because I have no idea what happened. In the 12 hours after I migrated all of Google to Google Calendar we had over a 1000 bugs filed by Google engineers and the bugs were things like: "The font is offset by one pixel on this screen after this 17-keystroke event." Engineers file good bugs. By being our own user we found bugs more quickly. We were able to find those errors and we created a whole internal market around incremental innovation.

On leadership and HR processes as innovation levers
Google had a big advantage. We were a greenfields operation. We created our culture. In places that didn't create our culture, there are only two levers you have to push.

If you look at the literature on business success and on military success, you'll find that almost everybody talks about leadership as the answer – leadership as the answer to everything. When I was a researcher at RAND I did a bunch of studies into, among other things, highly effective military units. And one of the things I found is that leadership does not appear to matter at all. Leadership appears to be completely a red herring on almost every front – except on one. Without strong leadership you will not build diverse teams; you will not hire diverse employees. If you do not hire diverse employees, you will not get multiple perspectives. If you do not get multiple perspectives, your innovation will die because you'll all see the problem the same way. Leadership is critical to building diversity and by extension innovation. Secondly, [look at] your HR processes. Probably you're compensating people and promoting them based on execution and execution alone. The problem with that is that risk-takers get the short end of the stick because risk-takers won't always "execute." So they won't get extra money and they won't get promoted. They'll just sort of lag. And soon they will learn that to get promoted and get more money, to get more important and get a corner office and a designated parking space, you must never try anything new. So if you're trying to become an innovative culture, these are your two levers.

Innovation is happening in your organization today. It's just that you're probably killing it. The odds are good. Left to its own devices, innovation is fragile; it will not survive. Your job as a leader is to find the innovations, foster them, and wait as long as you can to kill them. Because it's likely you'll kill the good ones. We tried to kill Gmail. We tried to kill AdSense. Because the really good ones are antithetical to what you know how to do. And you have to accept risk. You have to accept a tax for failure and treat it as an opportunity for learning.

[1] These quotes are transcribed and edited excerpts from a videotaped presentation by Douglas Merrill. The 55-minute talk can be found at http://www.youtube.com/watch?v=2GtgSkmDnbQ

The Lean Six Sigma way

Driving operational innovation

Dave Lubowe, George Byrne
and Amy Blitz

Finding ways to enable innovation remains a challenge for many CEOs. Top companies with successful track records of innovation, however, have discovered one possible solution. Lean Six Sigma, a relatively well-known approach for achieving operational efficiency, can do far more than simply improve processes.

Around the world CEOs are searching for blockbuster products and services, making major operational changes, and even redesigning their fundamental business models. This trend toward broad-based innovation was evident in *Expanding the Innovation Horizon*, which found that CEOs' innovation priorities were spread across all of these different dimensions (see Figure 1). And yet CEOs ranked an "unsupportive culture and climate" as their biggest obstacle to innovation success.[1] Their organizations lacked the processes, discipline and organizational mindset to foster meaningful innovation on a sustained basis.

Our research and experience show that the right operations strategy

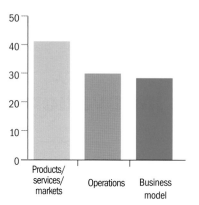

FIGURE 1. CEOs' innovation emphasis.
(Per cent of emphasis allocated to each innovation type)

Source: "Expanding the Innovation Horizon: The Global CEO Study 2006." IBM Global Business Services. March 2006.

can help companies make innovation a regular occurrence. Such a strategy, if focused not just on efficiency but also on growth, can serve as a foundation for innovation throughout an organization – far beyond operations to products, services, markets and even a company's underlying business model. Simply put, this sort of strategy is not about doing things better; it is about doing better things.

As part of our analysis, we examined several leading companies that are doing just that. They have implemented operations strategies based on a relatively well-known management philosophy, which we will call Lean Six Sigma. It is also sometimes referred to as Six Sigma Lean. And at some of the companies we studied, leaders still label their initiatives as Six Sigma or 6 Sigma even though, from our perspective, they have moved beyond Six Sigma's original definition and scope by incorporating Lean features as well.

Regardless of the term, the companies that have used this overall approach have established disciplined working environments focused on customer needs, detailed data analysis and facts, not theories. The results are remarkable:

• At Caterpillar, stagnant revenue growth prompted the company to undertake a massive transformation in January 2001. Through its 6 Sigma initiative, the company developed a strategic vision that outlined a roadmap for change based on fact-based analysis. Caterpillar's initiative also led to product innovations like its phenomenally successful low-emissions diesel engine and to redesigned processes including a streamlined supply chain. By 2005, revenues had grown by 80 per cent.

• Coddled by decades of government protection, Korean steelmaker POSCO faced fierce competition as it privatized in 2000. But with the help of Lean Six Sigma, the company staged a dramatic turnaround. This approach helped POSCO escape its low-margin business as a regional low-cost provider and elevate itself to the global stage as a premier provider of innovative steel products and services. In just a few short years as a private enterprise, POSCO has become the world's third-largest steelmaker.

- In a newly deregulated market, ScottishPower was losing customers who now had the power to choose their electricity provider. Determined to reverse the trend, the company used a Lean Six Sigma approach to reinvent its customer service function. By innovating based on facts not assumptions, the company was able to halt a steady decline in its customer base and increase market share by 60 per cent in just four years.

Although CEOs might instinctively think of management approaches such as Lean Six Sigma in terms of process improvement and cost reduction, our research suggests that this perspective is shortsighted. The successful companies we studied acted in a more visionary manner. They deliberately expanded the scope of Lean Six Sigma, using it to find significant innovation opportunities that affected much more than their operations.

The evolution of the Lean Six Sigma approach

As its name suggests, Lean Six Sigma is a combination of Lean methods and Six Sigma approaches. It builds on the knowledge, methods and tools derived from decades of operational improvement research and implementation (see Figure 2). Lean approaches focus on reducing cost through process optimization. Six Sigma is about meeting customer requirements and stakeholder expectations, and improving quality by measuring and eliminating defects. The Lean Six Sigma approach draws on the philosophies, principles and tools of both (see Figure 3).

In the past, companies used Lean Six Sigma primarily for operational improvement – refining existing processes to reduce costs, improve performance and provide better customer value. However, dramatic upheavals in the competitive marketplace are prompting business change on a much more massive scale. Companies must innovate, not just improve.

Despite its heritage, Lean Six Sigma is well suited for this change in target and scope. The leading companies we studied are proving that the Lean Six Sigma approach has applications far beyond process improvement; they are using it to innovate in all areas of their businesses – their operations, their products and services and even their business models.

FIGURE 2. **Lean Six Sigma builds on the practical lessons learned from previous eras of operational improvement.**

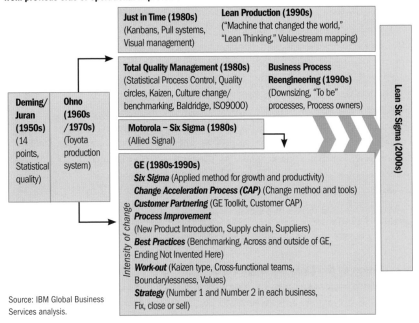

Source: IBM Global Business Services analysis.

FIGURE 3. **Lean Six Sigma incorporates, and deploys, the key methods, tools and techniques of its predecessors.**

Lean focuses on waste elimination in existing processes.

| **A**nalyze opportunity | **P**lan improvement | **F**ocus improvement | **D**eliver performance | **I**mprove performance |

Six Sigma focuses on Continuous Process Improvement (DMAIC) to reduce variation in existing processes.

| **D**efine opportunity | **M**easure performance | **A**nalyze opportunity | **I**mprove performance | **C**ontrol performance |

Six Sigma also focuses on New Process Design/Complete Redesign (DMEDI) for wholesale redesign of processes as well as new products and services.

| **D**efine opportunity | **M**easure requirements | **E**xplore solutions | **D**evelop solutions | **I**mplement solutions |

Because of its core tenets – analysis based on facts and direct customer input – Lean Six Sigma is equipped to facilitate a much broader transformation, helping a company rethink its entire business and create a more innovative climate.

The concept in action

In virtually every industry and across the public sector, the Lean Six Sigma approach has served as a catalyst for broad-scale innovation. Though the organizations we studied vary in terms of size and mission, they have all realized substantial benefits – even earning positive responses from the fickle financial markets. Their experiences provide valuable lessons for firms that want to cultivate an innovative mindset.

Innovation finds its legs at Caterpillar: In 2000, Caterpillar had stalled, with four years of flat revenues and intense competition that showed no signs of faltering. Determined to regain its industry leadership position and jump-start growth, the company deployed a Lean Six Sigma approach, or what they refer to as "6 Sigma," in January 2001. Caterpillar wanted to revolutionize not only the way its employees worked, but also their mindsets. The goal: continuous, customer-driven innovation. The magnitude of the planned transition was staggering: 27 separate business units and more than 72,000 employees who spoke multiple languages located on six continents.

The launch began with a nine-month training period for 4200 employees. These trained professionals – with varied backgrounds, from engineering to finance – then each led their own projects and served as mentors to the rest of the organization.

> "It is always about control. 6 Sigma forces you to have the processes and the people accountable to make sure the results are enduring."
>
> *Dave Burritt, Vice-President, Chief Financial Officer, Caterpillar* [2]

Perhaps the most far-reaching transformation came from applying 6 Sigma approaches to strategy development. Using these disciplines to collect and analyze hard data on customers, markets and Caterpillar's capabilities, the CEO and a strategic planning committee crafted a detailed vision for Caterpillar in 2020. The vision was subdivided into three five-year plans. The immediate plan set out specific, measurable targets for market position, quality, order-to-delivery performance, safety and other critical success factors. The plan was company-wide, spanning all lines of business and cascading down through the organization. Through the rigor and discipline enforced by the initiative, the entire company aligned itself behind the same specific objectives.

Engineer to engineer, Caterpillar employees and clients began working collaboratively to develop solutions.

The initial 6 Sigma launch spawned more than 1100 projects – some generated subtle (though financially beneficial) operational improvements, while others resulted in innovative new products and radically different ways of working. One of the first process changes involved revamping R&D to include more direct interaction with the customer. Engineer to engineer, employees and clients began working collaboratively to pinpoint problems and develop solutions, steadily building closer relationships.

Through alliances it built with Canadian mining customers, for example, Caterpillar learned about the nuances involved in extracting oil from sand. These application-specific insights led the company to develop a completely different kind of mining truck. Instead of offering a "one-size-fits-all" model, its new mining truck is available in five configurations – each suited to a particular type of terrain and haul profile. Now, customers in extremely cost-sensitive industries can select the configuration that offers the best blend of price and productivity.

Teams also developed a tremendously successful diesel engine breakthrough that set Caterpillar apart from competitors. The ACERT® Technology significantly reduces emissions and offers higher fuel efficiency, saving customers money and allowing the company to command premium pricing.

This approach also led to major operational changes, particularly in Caterpillar's supply chain. Caterpillar has, in its own words, "systematically de-bottlenecked" its order-to-delivery process. For example, teams redesigned the production scheduling process at Caterpillar manufacturing facilities, cutting lead times by more than 50 per cent. They have also reduced delays caused by supplier-sourced pumps. Historically, if a pump failed during initial testing, Caterpillar had to fix the pump or wait for the supplier to send someone to repair it. Now, based on suggestions from the 6 Sigma team, the supplier has its own pump test cell and breaks in new pumps before sending them to Caterpillar plants. And the supplier faces a financial penalty if it fails to meet specific quality goals.

STRONG LEADERSHIP YIELDS SPEED AND STRATEGIC ALIGNMENT

Applying Lean Six Sigma to strategy development sends a clear message about how serious management teams are about making an enduring change.

In the case of Caterpillar, strong leadership prompted strong participation, unifying 27 disparate organizational units around common strategic goals. Teams saw how their efforts were linked and contributed to the whole. Results were measurable and visible to all. While its 6 Sigma initiative helped make the changes enduring, strong leadership and broad participation made them happen fast. Caterpillar recouped its initial investment in less than a year.

Overall, the results from Caterpillar's initiative have been phenomenal. Caterpillar launched 6 Sigma globally and delivered benefits that surpassed implementation costs in the first year. Since then, it has become a critical component of Caterpillar's success. The rigor and discipline have enabled the record profits of the past few years and are helping the company achieve its 2010 strategic goals. According to Caterpillar Vice-President and CFO Dave Burritt, "Caterpillar's competitiveness has improved ... 6 Sigma has been applied to increase our [percentage] of industry in all of our principal lines of business. The machine, the engine and financial products businesses have all benefited from the rigor of 6 Sigma. Without question, we are in the best of times at Caterpillar, and the improvements would have been much less without 6 Sigma."[3]

POSCO shines in lackluster steel industry: After decades of government ownership, the Korean steel company POSCO was privatized in 2000. Long sheltered from market forces, the company suddenly faced serious competitive pressures. In particular, its low-cost competitive advantage was evaporating as cheaper competitors emerged from other regions, notably China. Its limited regional footprint also left the company exposed to a declining Korean economy.

Undaunted, POSCO was determined to remake itself, shifting from a local, low-cost producer to a global, value-added steel maker. To do so, its entire way of working had to change. The company made a fundamental commitment to use a Lean Six Sigma approach to transform its business and create a market-driven mindset throughout the enterprise.[5]

Initially, R&D resisted the Lean Six Sigma approach, feeling it was too Western to be practical for an Asian company. But after special training sessions, designed with these engineers in mind, opinions began to shift. Instead of sending marketing or salespeople to research customer needs, senior management sent engineers. This empowered the people who were making the pivotal design decisions to talk directly with key customers and make recommendations. For the engineers, this approach provided opportunities to learn directly from customers.

> POSCO was in a difficult situation – you might almost say a crisis – a few years ago as we faced this new global competitive threat ... we felt that Six Sigma was a good vehicle to change all employees' way of thinking ...
>
> *Ku-taek Lee, Chairman and CEO, POSCO[4]*

As the POSCO management team developed its strategy for becoming a value-added rather than a low-cost steel provider, it again relied on Lean Six Sigma. Using the engineering team's input on customer needs, senior management analyzed market potential and the company's capabilities in those product and service areas. The optimal strategy seemed to revolve around two high-potential markets: shipping and automotive. Senior managers then aligned the entire company behind these strategic priorities. R&D concentrated on these two areas, and pet projects that did not contribute to the value-added vision were cancelled. (It's important to note that these priorities were not static. With Lean Six Sigma helping POSCO maintain a perpetual watch over customer needs and market opportunities, the company has since added a construction vertical to the mix.)

The business model shift to focus on the shipping and automotive

INNOVATION DOMINO EFFECT

As Lean Six Sigma disciplines steadily infiltrates the thought processes of employees and company leaders, they create a domino effect of innovation. In the case of POSCO, as the company innovated in one area of the business, it triggered transformation in another. For example, the business model decision to focus on high-potential segments such as the automotive industry inspired new, innovative steel products. These new products, in turn, led to new processes to produce higher-grade steel.

Collectively, these ripples of innovation enabled POSCO to accomplish a top-to-bottom transformation – from government-owned business to profitable private enterprise; from low-cost producer to value-added provider; and from regional player to global competitor.

industries led to major product innovations. For example, the company invented steel that remains rust-free in salt water, creating significant opportunities in shipping and floating dock construction.

Using Lean Six Sigma to drive interactions with global car manufacturers, POSCO developed 21 varieties of high-grade steel to meet special industry needs, such as coated steel that paint adheres to more easily.

> ... POSCO had transformed itself from a regional, low-cost producer to a global, value-added provider of high-quality steel. It is now the third-largest steelmaker worldwide.

Lean Six Sigma analysis soon led to another realization: in order to expand its products and markets, POSCO would have to expand its operations as well. Although China is the world's biggest producer of steel (and therefore a competitive threat), the expanding gap between its own production capabilities and rapidly rising demand provided a growth opportunity for POSCO. To fill this gap, POSCO has orchestrated 14 joint ventures and invested $US780 million in China. Just a decade ago, that investment figure was zero.[6]

Using Lean Six Sigma's relentless focus on customer demands, POSCO developed process and IT innovations that dramatically reduced finished steel inventories and cut lead times from 28 days to just 14 by 2003.[7] At the same time, however, the company's focus on customer needs sometimes created additional challenges. For example, POSCO found that filling orders faster left too many partly used steel slabs, which hurt margins. Determined to meet customer needs profitably, POSCO developed sophisticated production scheduling algorithms that allowed it to pack multiple orders on a slab. This allowed the company to optimize slab utilization (and profitability), while still responding rapidly to customer demand.[8]

In addition to growth and profitability, the Lean Six Sigma approach helped POSCO realize an altruistic objective – to help restore and protect Korea's natural environment. The years after the Korean War were hard on Korea ecologically; in the drive to improve economic conditions, companies too often ignored the environmental effects of their actions. In an effort to contribute positively in this area, POSCO, through its Lean Six Sigma efforts, was able to introduce diverse environmental management programs and processes, including an iron-making approach that eliminates the sintering and coking processes, which, in turn, reduces environmental pollutants.

As the Lean Six Sigma way of thinking spread across POSCO, virtually no area of the business was off-limits. The company was equally comfortable (and confident) applying the approach to corporate strategy and budgeting as to manufacturing and logistics.

Through its Lean Six Sigma efforts, POSCO has produced more than $US1 billion in financial gains to date, including strong savings and record sales volumes. Even in 2001, the first year of its Lean Six Sigma initiative, when 25-year lows in prices hit other steelmakers and their investors hard, POSCO achieved double-digit profitability.[9] By 2005, in less than four years, the company had transformed itself from a regional, low-cost producer to a global, value-added provider of high-quality steel. POSCO is now the third-largest steelmaker worldwide. It also ranks high in terms of efficiency and profitability and has been selected as "the world's most competitive steel firm" for three consecutive years in a global study conducted by World Steel Dynamics.[10]

A ScottishPower Play: In 2001, ScottishPower found itself losing market share in the recently deregulated UK retail energy marketplace. Regulators who were responsible for a safe, reliable energy supply were beginning to express concern about recurring customer service complaints. The company needed to reverse the trend quickly. By radically overhauling its customer service and sales operations, it hoped to regain a market-leading position.

Defying the notion that Lean Six Sigma is primarily for manufacturing firms, ScottishPower decided to use the approach to drive innovation in its services-based business. It launched Lean Six Sigma by establishing a Business Transformation Department and training hundreds of employees.

Very quickly, the Lean Six Sigma approach proved that the company's initial assumptions about why customers were leaving were off-base. In reality, many customers were being lost when they moved to a different home. When customers called to cancel their service, customer service representatives (CSRs) did just that, following their scripts precisely but never considering whether the caller might need service elsewhere. They were extremely efficient, but not effective. Once Lean Six Sigma exposed this market-share leak, ScottishPower instituted a "hot key" process to transfer callers to advisers who could offer service at the caller's new home. The company also offered financial incentives to CSRs to encourage the transfers. Because Lean

Six Sigma forced an end-to-end inspection, ScottishPower was able to close the loop by designing a new process that notified sales teams to approach the new inhabitants at the vacated address. So instead of losing a customer, the firm was now more likely to end up with two.

In its initial wave, ScottishPower launched 130 such Lean Six Sigma projects. Others included a targeted marketing campaign that boosted use of direct debit payments by 14 per cent, a simplified sign-up process for business customers that led to a 20 per cent increase in acquisition, and new meter reading processes with lower costs and higher accuracy.

FACTS TRUMP ASSUMPTIONS

Lean Six Sigma focuses on facts. For ScottishPower, Lean Six Sigma helped them identify the real reasons for customer dissatisfaction and defection. The company no longer needed to rely on guesses or assumptions – it had facts. With these insights, the company was able to redesign the specific processes that affected customer relationships. And in the end, the cost of regaining its market share through Lean Six Sigma was much lower than a traditional mass-marketing approach.

Combined, the Lean Six Sigma approach helped ScottishPower expand from 3.2 million to 5.1 million customers in just four years, or an average of about 40,000 new customers per month during the period. This contrasts sharply with the trend of declining numbers of customers for many of ScottishPower's competitors. These gains are even more remarkable given that all of these companies are competing in the same market for a relatively stable number of households. To date, ScottishPower has realized a total of $US170 million in additional revenue and cost savings through its Lean Six Sigma initiatives.

> ... The Lean Six Sigma approach helped ScottishPower expand from 3.2 million to 5.1 million customers in just four years, or an average of about 40,000 new customers per month during the period.

Assess your own innovative climate

The successful companies we studied took a deliberate detour from the traditional approach to operational improvement. By using the Lean Six Sigma approach in a broader, more strategic fashion, they were able to uncover innovation opportunities across their business –

IT'S NOT JUST FOR THE PRIVATE SECTOR

The Lean Six Sigma approach can also be applied to the challenges of the public sector. Take, for example, the Office of the Principal Legal Advisor (OPLA) in the U.S. Department of Homeland Security Bureau of Immigration and Customs Enforcement. OPLA, the department's largest legal program, litigates 400,000 alien removal cases each year. Embracing strategic management and Lean Six Sigma, it deployed a nationwide, web-accessible case and document management system; gave each employee a scanner; established a Strategic Review Division to review offices and spread best practices; improved hiring and training; and formed numerous Lean Six Sigma working groups made up of employees from across the country.

By giving its employees shared ownership in processes, OPLA is quickly moving toward more efficient litigation and administrative processes – improving the electronic exchange of documents with the private bar; increasing the efficiency with which court cases are calendared; devising case-management metrics that will capture inefficiencies in its litigation processes; and creating electronic case files that its trial attorneys can carry into courtrooms on laptops. Many other processes are under review, and OPLA is forming strategic alliances with stakeholder agencies. With software enhancements, new personnel, and numerous process fixes in the works, OPLA will continue its transformation. Lean Six Sigma has been key to its success.

not just in operations. And in the process, they were able to improve business performance and establish organizations that are more naturally inclined to innovate.

As we analyzed their Lean Six Sigma efforts, we identified several distinguishing features of their approaches that set them apart from those with a traditional operational improvement mindset. The common characteristics shared by these innovators include:

- An innovation vision based on factual customer and market insights – leaders crafted a compelling vision based on a keen understanding of market demands and their own capabilities. Their objectives were explicit and few in number to enable focus.
- Leadership committed to perpetual innovation – CEOs and business unit leaders played active, enthusiastic roles. They were clearly committed to making an indelible cultural change, not just launching another initiative.
- Alignment across the extended enterprise – the strategic innovation vision was used as a unifying force to align disparate business units and influence supplier and customer relationships.
- Organizational capabilities that made innovation habitual – at the

outset, these companies' Lean Six Sigma initiatives involved an intense period of training, dedicated resources and an initial bubble of projects to jump-start their transformation. But over time, as the mindset became more mainstream, these companies established enduring processes that helped drive innovation throughout the organization.

The challenges these companies faced are not unique. Peers around the world are feeling similar pressure to innovate. The pivotal question is whether your organization is equipped to do so – and to do so in a sustainable manner. Here are several questions that can help you assess your level of preparedness:

- Do you have a clear vision of where you want your company to be in two years? In five years? In 10 years?
- How closely tied is this vision to the needs of your existing and target customers? And is your understanding of these needs based on actual assessments or assumed information?
- Will this vision require innovations in your business model? In your products or services? In your markets?
- What will you need to do at the operational level to enable and drive these innovations?
- To support innovation, what changes will be required to your management approach, organizational structures, metrics and skills?
- How are you making innovation happen more systematically? Are you establishing the right environment?

Conclusion

CEOs might be tempted to downplay the importance of operations strategy and related management approaches such as Lean Six Sigma, thinking of them in terms of process improvement and cost reduction. But this perspective is competitively shortsighted. Industry leaders – such as the companies analyzed in our study – are using Lean Six Sigma approaches to reveal significant innovation opportunities with far-reaching effects on their businesses. Certainly their operations are changing dramatically – but so are their products and services, their target markets and, in some cases, even the fundamental design of their business models.

Most importantly, the successes of the companies we researched were not anomalies. Through the discipline of Lean Six Sigma, these CEOs and business unit leaders have substantially improved business performance and permanently reoriented their organizations' mindsets, creating the type of environment where innovation can flourish.

About the authors

Dave Lubowe is Global and Americas Operations Strategy Leader for IBM Global Business Services. He can be contacted at dave.lubowe@us.ibm.com.

George Byrne is a former Americas Group Lean Six Sigma Leader for IBM Global Business Services.

Amy Blitz is Strategy and Change Leader at the IBM Institute for Business Value. She can be contacted at ablitz@us.ibm.com.

Contributors

Saul Berman is Global and Americas Business Strategy Leader for IBM Global Business Services. He can be reached at saul.berman@us.ibm.com.

Ian Wilson is Global Lean Six Sigma Leader and Operations Strategy Leader for Europe with IBM Global Business Services. He can be reached at ian.b.wilson@uk.ibm.com.

We would also like to thank other contributors, including Paul Campbell-Kelly, Jerry Coover, Geoff Gibbons, Changdae Kim, Bill Kane, Mark McDonald, and many others throughout IBM, all of whom generously shared their time and insights to help produce this paper.

References

[1] "Expanding the Innovation Horizon: The Global CEO Study 2006." IBM Business Consulting Services. March 2006. http://www.ibm.com/bcs/ceostudy

[2] IBM Global Business Services interview with Mr. Burritt, March 31, 2006.

[3] IBM Global Business Services correspondence with Mr. Burritt, August 3, 2006.

[4] "The Gartner Fellows Interviews: Ku-taek Lee, Chief Executive Officer, POSCO." Gartner, Inc. April 12, 2005.
http://bvit2.gartner.com/research/fellows/asset_140300_1176.jsp.

[5] Because POSCO launched its transformation efforts before the term "Lean Six Sigma" came into common use, it continues to refer to it as Six Sigma.

[6] Brooke, James, "Korean Steel Maker Finds Strength in Flexibility." *New York Times*, August 5, 2003.

[7] Ibid.

[8] IBM Corporation. "Optimizing production scheduling helps POSCO to meet new customer demands and reduce costs."
http://domino.research.ibm.com/odis/odis.nsf/pages/case.12.html

[9] Brooke, James, "Korean Steel Maker Finds Strength in Flexibility." *New York Times*, August 5, 2003.

[10] Ibid. Keun-min, Bae. "POSCO World's Most Competitive Steel Firm." *The Korea Times*. June 20, 2004.

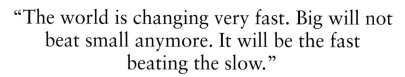

"The world is changing very fast. Big will not beat small anymore. It will be the fast beating the slow."

Rupert Murdoch, Chairman and CEO, News Corporation

"Business innovation - changing companies for a changing world." Principal Voices.
http://www.principalvoices.com/business.html

Speaking of innovation 4

PETER FARRELL is the founder and CEO of ResMed, a leading medical technology company specializing in the treatment and management of sleep-disordered breathing (SDB). Formed in 1989 and now headquartered in San Diego, California, ResMed operates in 80 countries though most of its sales are in the Americas (53 per cent), Germany (14 per cent) and France (13 per cent). In 2006, *Forbes* recognized ResMed as one of the 200 Best Small Companies in the US for the 10th year in a row. In 2005, Dr Farrell was named US National Entrepreneur of the Year in Health Sciences.

Q: How much emphasis does your company place on innovation?
A: First, we have no choice other than to keep innovating across the board. It doesn't matter who you ask, whether it's Jeffrey Immelt at General Electric or Ed Zander at Motorola, we all know that when you have the cost structures we have in the developed world, if you don't innovate, you're dead. But there has to be an economic dimension – if no one writes a check, innovation does not exist. Innovation has to be confirmed by the marketplace, it's that simple. It's when we bring out new products that you see a jump in our revenues. People think: "Oh my God, they've got it solved. That's what I want."

Q: What role do your customers play?
A: You have to keep incredibly close to your customers. But you need to examine what they say very carefully. Customers tend to look through the rear-view mirror. They think about what they're using today and say, "Here's what we'd like to see." So yes, you ask them what they'd like, but you've got to sift through those responses to find the people who actually get what you're doing. Think in terms of the Pareto Principle – that 20 per cent of your customers will give you 80 per cent of your revenues. You can apply that to lots of things. So we take it further to a sort of double Pareto (80 per cent of 80 and 20 per cent of 20). So that 64 per cent of your revenues and 64 per cent of your good ideas are likely to come from 4 per cent of your customers. Those sophisticated customers – often found in academe – are at the leading edge, they have great ideas

and they know where the area's going. The others will most likely give you information based on a relatively trivial understanding. So it's that really creative 4 per cent who can think about the future that you need to listen to. Then we balance that with our own technology-driven activities. We have plenty of good ideas internally, which customers wouldn't really be in a position to evaluate because they're too leading-edge.

Q: ResMed has had 18 years of continuous growth. How has the change from six employees when you started to 3000 now affected your ability to innovate?
A: The bigger you get, the more bureaucracy you end up with. And it becomes very, very hard to maintain a culture of innovation because people think: "Oh my God, there'll be so many of these, we have to get it right." And that's true. But you also have to be agile and quick. So you constantly have to take a machete to the bureaucracy. Unfortunately the people who come in see a big company – which we are, relatively speaking. I think once you get beyond 500 people, it's hard to stay nimble and quick. Ideally you'd like to work in pockets of a couple of hundred. So fighting bureaucracy is vital and you simply have to keep working at it.

Q: Where are your innovative energies focused?
A: First, we must keep innovating our products. Our algorithms, our masks and so on, everything is superb. But we must keep coming up with technology that's smaller, quieter, lighter, more user-friendly and which people will pay for.

And we have to keep looking at our processes. When you're moving 325,000 masks a month and 80,000 machines, there are lots of ways you can save money by supply chain management and so on.

But we really need to be creative and innovative in terms of how we look at the marketplace and how we get to customers. We know we have a huge area to cover. The prevalence of sleep-disordered breathing (SDB) is very high – 20 per cent of all adults suffer from this disease. That is a monster number and it means there's a monster market. SDB affects so many medical silos. But in a way our biggest competitor is ignorance.

Eighty per cent of Type II diabetes sufferers have SDB. But they don't know it because their physicians don't know it. So do half of cardiac patients, yet the cardiologists don't see it. Forty per cent of hypertension patients have SDB and there are 65 million of them. And so on. How do you get access to these people?

Look at the average profile of a trucker: he eats horse manure, drinks like a fish, doesn't exercise, works long hours and takes uppers and downers. Ninety-three per cent of them are male and 50 per cent of them have SDB. Almost a third of them have it at a level that threatens to cause accidents. So we got involved in a pilot study with Schneider National, a trucking company in Green Bay, Wisconsin. In that 18-month study, the use of SDB diagnosis and subsequent treatment in several hundred drivers resulted in a saving of $6500 per driver per year in direct medical expenses, a 30 per cent reduction in accidents, and a 229 per cent improvement in retention of drivers. And training and retention of drivers are the biggest problems facing trucking companies. Schneider has now made the assessment of a driver's level of SDB mandatory. And, if anyone has it at a significant level, he or she must undergo treatment.

So we don't really know how big this market can be and we have to find innovative ways to deal with the problem.

We have to think about how we deal with market structures that are so grossly inefficient and so grossly ignorant. How can we change that paradigm in ways that help us drive the business more cost-effectively? If we can innovate there, and get the cash flow coming in, then that allows us to open up bigger silos to milk. This is a marathon and we're just lacing our shoes.

"The aspect of innovation most exciting to me, and the one most critical to this industry, is the broad collaboration required to make an idea a reality."

Rashid Skaf, President and CEO, AMX Corporation

Skaf, Rashid. "Passion for Innovation." Residential Systems. November 4, 2005.
http://resmagonline.com/articles/publish/article_988.shtml

The new rules of Value 2.0

How to capitalize on emerging technologies

Matt Porta, Brian House, Lisa Buckley and Amy Blitz

We stand at the dawn of an era of transformational change. The Internet, globalization and innovative new technologies are coming together in ways that are changing the rules of business, culture and society. The purpose of this chapter is to help executives understand how emerging technologies and principles are enabling value creation through what we call the "new rules of Value 2.0."

Our research shows that while we are living in an era of vast opportunity for innovation and growth, executives are deeply concerned about their organizations' ability to capitalize on this transformation. A staggering two-thirds of the CEOs interviewed in *Expanding the Innovation Horizon* said that they needed to make fundamental changes to their businesses within the next two years.[1]

They know the rules are changing. A company like Craigslist can create and run a site that serves 5 billion page views per month – and is one of the 40 most visited sites in the world – with only 24 employees.[2] Meanwhile, companies like Apple (iTunes) are disrupting industry value chains with innovative business models. Those who ignore these transformations do so at their peril. Those who understand and leverage Value 2.0 approaches will be postitioned to capture real value.

The enabling technologies behind Value 2.0 are the emerging technologies of Web 2.0, social computing, service-oriented architecture, 3D Internet, and virtual worlds. The focus of this paper is not on the new technologies *per se*, but on how businesses are using them to improve performance and enable new means of value creation.

In particular, we wanted to find out whether these new rules of value creation were applicable to large enterprises. So we examined more than 100 start-ups and 40 large enterprises to see how they were leveraging emerging technologies to create value. Using publicly available information to assess these companies, we identified eight new rules of Value 2.0. We then polled more than 500 experts – technology analysts, IBM business leaders and top venture capitalists – to gather their insights on how these emerging technologies will evolve and which aspects of Value 2.0 hold the most significant opportunities for large enterprises.

As a harbinger of disruptive change in business, billions of dollars have flowed into start-ups focused on emerging technologies. These

Figure 1. New rules of Value 2.0.

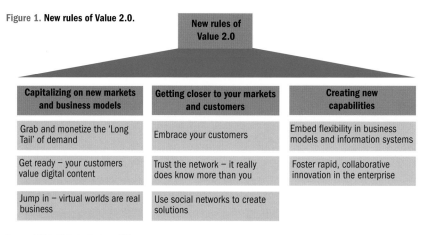

Source: IBM Institute for Business Value.

businesses have used such technologies to change the way companies and customers interact, and have developed new business models to support this. The question is: Do any of their business models or approaches to value creation apply to large enterprises? The answer is a definite "yes."

The new rules of Value 2.0 fall into three broad categories (see Figure 1). These rules illustrate different ways in which emerging technologies are enabling new value creation in the enterprise. Of the start-ups and large enterprises we examined, innovative large enterprises tended to experiment with multiple new rules of Value 2.0, while technology start-ups tended to focus on one or two new rules (see Figure 2).

Our study found that large enterprises focused primarily on Value 2.0 in the context of customer intimacy, solutions and social networking. Start-ups, on the other hand, leaned more toward exploiting "long tail" economics and meeting underserved market segments. Both groups, however, had a significant focus on value created by harnessing network intelligence (see Figure 3). These results were echoed by the responses to our informal poll of IBM business and technology leaders.

Figure 2. Number of new rules exhibited by start-ups and large enterprises.

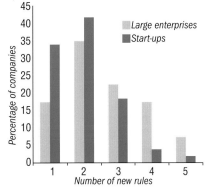

Source: IBM Institute for Business Value.
Note: Companies may exhibit more than one new rule; no company exhibited more than five new rules.

Figure 3. Percentage of start-ups and large enterprises exhibiting particular new rules.

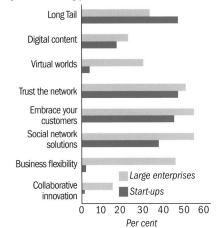

Source: IBM Institute for Business Value.
Note: Sum of percentages is greater than 100% as companies may exhibit more than one new rule.

Capitalizing on new markets and business models

The first three new rules focus on expanding into new markets and creating new business models. In essence, they hold the potential to capitalize on emerging market opportunities, develop new revenue streams and increase market share. Now is the time for enterprises to enter these markets, adjust their business model as necessary, and secure first-mover advantage.

RULE #1: Grab and monetize the "long tail"

For many enterprises the Pareto Principle or "80/20 rule" is a fundamental business principle. Enterprises tend to focus on the roughly 20 per cent of their customers or product mix that generates 80 per cent of their revenue or profit. Enterprises have known for a long time that a very broad product selection is not cost-effective – shelf space and inventory costs are too high. Therefore marketing efforts are geared toward the critical 20 per cent. This cycle is, of course, self-reinforcing. If you offer only a limited range of products and services, people will buy only those products and services. Value 2.0 challenges the 80/20 rule.

As Chris Anderson discussed in *The Long Tail*, new technologies have lowered both the cost of accessing customers and the cost of offering a much wider selection of goods and services.[3] Grabbing and monetizing the long tail of demand – beyond the core 20 per cent – applies to both start-ups and large enterprises. For start-ups, a focus on the long tail of demand in their industries has already proved effective. Threadless, for example, enables its customers to design their own T-shirt which is produced, marketed and sold in very small batches, and comes complete with recommendations and ratings. Another start-up, Saltworks.com, offers more than 100 gourmet salts at competitive prices – many more than the typical dozen or so found in the best gourmet stores.[4]

Amazon.com has demonstrated that large enterprises can generate real value using this kind of approach. Lowered search costs enabled by social recommendation engines as well as community marketing effects are ways in which emerging technologies have enabled Amazon.com to pursue this strategy. The value created speaks for itself – nearly 25-30 per cent of Amazon.com's book sales are titles you won't find in a typical "bricks and mortar" store.[5]

This genie will not go back into the bottle – the enabling technologies behind Amazon.com's success are available to all enterprises. Indeed, these technologies are changing customer expectations and purchase behaviors across industries. Customers are increasingly uninterested in settling for a less than ideal product, service or solution. Enterprises that understand and act on this change are more likely to reap the rewards of Value 2.0. Figure 2 shows that while less than one-third of the large enterprises studied were experimenting with value creation based on this rule, nearly half of the start-ups we analyzed were doing so.

RULE #2: Your customers value digital content

Emerging technologies are enabling new ways to create, share and consume all forms of digital content. This shift is causing dramatic changes in many established business models and opening up entirely new markets. Forward-thinking enterprises can take advantage of this by adjusting their business models and business design. However, this is not easy. In our research, only 23 per cent of the large enterprises and 17 per cent of the start-ups were attempting to create value based on this rule.

The music industry is a poster child of this trend. Much has been written on how new technologies are breaking down the traditional bi-directional, pay-for-use industry model. While this has been viewed as a threat by the traditional music industry, overall music consumption is actually growing. People are listening everywhere – in gyms, planes, parks, shopping malls. Additionally, music is being accessed through all sorts of devices, from MP3 players to phones to laptops. Consumers are finding value in the ubiquity and liquidity of their digital music, and therein lies the business opportunity – even as industry value is being visibly (and often painfully) redistributed to those companies able to reconfigure themselves.

New business models are emerging. Prince gave away his "*Planet Earth*" album to several hundred thousand British fans who purchased the *Mail on Sunday* newspaper.[6] Radiohead released its recent album "In Rainbows" over the web, with a "name your own price" model for fans (down to and including a price of $0).[7] Both Prince and Radiohead are using these giveaways to stimulate demand and buzz, with the objective of generating substantial revenue through tours and limited-edition content sold at a premium.

This new rule does not apply only to the entertainment industry. Digitization is expanding across diverse industries. For example Motorcycle fans can download professional promotional videos of their bikes and ring tones that capture the sound of their bike's acceleration. Or they can share their own videos with other enthusiasts or even buy a virtual bike in Second Life. Although many companies do not yet realize it, these digital product extensions can be very valuable; in some cases they can be worth more than the physical product.[8]

While this trend does not currently apply equally to every industry, within many markets it is a real and significant opportunity for innovative enterprises. The race is on for enterprises to develop their innovative capacities and organizational abilities, to change their business models, and to capture Value 2.0 generated by ubiquitous digital content.

RULE #3: Virtual worlds are real business

Virtual worlds and other three-dimensional online environments were born in the massively multiplayer online game (MMOG) arena. However, they have quickly evolved to become one of the hottest areas of Value 2.0. It is estimated that investors have put more than $US1 billion into virtual worlds since October 2006.[9]

It has been fairly easy for large enterprises to enter this space and explore value creation. Our analysis showed that nearly 30 per cent of sampled large enterprises were leveraging virtual worlds, while only 4 per cent of the start-ups were doing so. Virtual worlds have a variety of potential applications and exciting business opportunities for large enterprises. These applications are enabling Value 2.0 in three broad areas:

• *Creating new markets for virtual products and services.* The visual, social and entertainment aspects of virtual worlds have created an entirely new market for virtual goods and services paid for in real-world dollars. These include clothing for your Avatar, virtual houses, cars and more, with total spending on virtual goods estimated at more than $US1.5 billion per year.[10] The popularity of virtual worlds has also enabled some companies to sell virtual products that complement or enhance real-world products, making their overall brand experience "longer and stronger" (for example, Mattel's Barbie).

• *Opening a richer direct channel to customers.* Virtual worlds such as Second Life represent a new channel to customers and provide new opportunities to advertise and market real-world products/ services. The interactivity and social aspects of this medium provide for extra value in customer interaction, beyond that of a simple web page or B2C/B2B site. This provides a direct channel to customers more akin to what channel partners and retailers have traditionally offered in the real world, further disrupting the value chain.

- *Enhancing collaboration and communication.* As MIT's Professor Irving Wladawsky-Berger stated at a recent conference, "Meetings and learning and training may very well be the 'killer app' for virtual worlds."[11] Enterprises are becoming increasingly more distributed across geographies. Their knowledge ecosystem is becoming fragmented across employees, partners and customers. To thrive in this hyper-distributed world, an enterprise needs to help ensure that its employees connect and collaborate. Face-to-face meetings are expensive and time-consuming, yet conference calls lose much in the way of the social capital created through personal interactions. Telepresence is one way to bridge this gap. Telepresence refers to a set of emerging technologies that help connect people by allowing them to feel that they are physically present at another location.[12] For example, IBM is holding new employee training sessions in Second Life in order to allow employees to "meet" in a virtual world. The goal is to offer a richer experience than a conference call.

  Simultaneously, advances in video-streaming are being used to support virtual collaboration. Cisco, for example, has launched telepresence products that take the old video-conference room to new levels of performance.[13] Since 3D worlds and video-streaming are both converging in this space, many experts see a combination of both video and 3D internet technologies as providing the best platform for virtual communication and collaboration via telepresence.

Getting closer to your markets and customers

The next set of rules illustrates how large enterprises can create new value with emerging technologies by becoming more intimate with customers, gaining better information and insight from the social Internet, and forming community experience around customer solutions.

RULE #4: The network really does know more than you

The Internet offers deep, broad and widely accessible information. And businesses are learning to tap this information source in new ways. Of the large enterprises we studied, 50 per cent were addressing value creation by tapping into network intelligence, while nearly 47 per cent of start-ups were creating value in a similar way.

If Web 1.0 was about putting basic product information on the internet, then Web 2.0 is about a rich commentary on all things by almost everyone, including consumers, experts, trendsetters, the average person and the not-so-average.

Mining this information for business intelligence and insight is just beginning. Emerging Web analytics technologies are making it possible to obtain much more valuable insights from the social Internet and the rich heterogeneous data produced by online social networks. Large enterprises need to recognize that this intelligence exists, often outside their current knowledge sources. But they must also have the right mindset, processes and tools in order to tap into, accept and act upon the wisdom of the masses.

There are many valid privacy concerns that will need to be addressed as this area matures. But the new, more socially interactive Internet is a tremendously valuable source of information on customers, markets, competitors, and other key concerns for a business. Enterprises that move quickly here will be rewarded with superior insights on sales and market trends, new product ideas, competitive intelligence and operational issues.

RULE #5: Embrace your customers

Staying close to your customers has been a classic business battle cry. Leading organizations have historically sought customer input in every stage of the life-cycle – from design to marketing to distribution and sales to after-sales support. Traditional ways to engage customers – focus groups, surveys and industry experts – are expensive and limited. Today's emerging technologies enable a new level of customer intimacy by changing the way enterprises connect and build customer relationships. Enterprises can move from knowing the customer to truly embracing the customer. This is another rule of value creation that is getting substantial attention, both in large enterprises and start-ups: Our analysis found that 55 per cent of large enterprises and 45 per cent of start-ups were creating Value 2.0 by embracing customers.

First, emerging technologies enable greater customer intimacy by increasing the ease of access to customers and lowering the relationship barrier. Customers are already online and many are discussing and commenting on every aspect of products and services. Enterprises that encourage free-form discussion around their products and services can start building a rich community of participation. Value 2.0 is then created as enterprises leverage this participation from customers to provide real-time input.

Emerging technologies can also create new value through customer intimacy via "crowdsourcing" and "crowdsupport." These terms refer to enlisting customers to help your enterprise directly in every aspect of the life-cycle. In the consumer world of Web 2.0, an organization like Wikipedia and virtual worlds have been able to leverage the small group of users willing to give their time and energy to create content for the larger community to use. This same principle applies to crowdsourcing and crowdsupport. A large enterprise can enlist its small group of highly dedicated users to help improve the overall quality of its products and services for all – and often these users will do it free of charge. For example, Nintendo has had great success with a program, described in detail below, that engages its dedicated users in all aspect of its business from design to customer support.[14]

As emerging technologies make it easier to connect with customers, it becomes easier for enterprises to find and encourage those small groups of highly dedicated users willing to help other users get the most out of these sites – to advocate the brand, spread the word, and contribute content to make the product/service/solution even more valuable. Nintendo's success indicates that this is as true for large enterprises as for the start-up or pure-play Internet company.

The result of this phenomenon, embracing the willingness of some customers to support a business directly, is Value 2.0 through better product/service/solution quality, a better brand experience and reduced costs to serve new customers with a richer interface. It is expected to remain a win-win relationship for both enterprises and their customers.

RULE #6: Use social networks to create solutions

Selling business solutions instead of products or services alone is an established strategy of many large enterprises. Solutions require better integration across business partners to meet client needs. That is why creating business ecosystem solutions through social networks is a new rule of Value 2.0.

Apple's iPod is the foremost example for this socially driven, Web-based ecosystem solution. In creating iTunes, Apple integrated content, devices and community into a business model. Combining all elements of the music ecosystem in one solution gave Apple a true competitive advantage, and helped Apple secure 70 per cent of the PC-based digital music market.[15]

Social networks, enabled by innovative technologies, are critical components for creating these Web-based solutions. As the previous rule showed, online social networks empower loyal brand advocates to enrich the user community. More specifically, social networks can drive value in these key areas:

- Building loyalty, trust and camaraderie in an increasingly mobile and global marketplace;
- Fostering innovative discussion and support among online communities with committed participants, expert users and early adopters; and
- Creating advocates for the company in the increasingly transparent world of the social Web, where information and misinformation disperses instantaneously.

With global competitive pressures increasing, large enterprises are taking this rule of Value 2.0 to heart. Our research found that 55 per cent of large enterprises were exploring Value 2.0 through social networks and corresponding ecosystem solutions. Among start-ups, 37 per cent were leveraging this new rule to create value.

Creating new capabilities

This next set of new rules focuses on Value 2.0 created by using emerging technologies inside the enterprise to build capability. Flexibility of business models and systems is becoming a critical aspect of creating value, especially as disruptive forces incapacitate existing enterprise models. Fostering rapid, collaborative innovation is another key theme to staying competitive, and another way in which emerging technologies are enabling Value 2.0.

RULE #7: Embed flexibility in business models and information systems

Traditional business models, processes and information systems have been built to be as highly efficient and effective as possible, but the ability to adapt quickly has not always been a top requirement. Not surprisingly, this new rule applies mostly to large enterprises, as start-ups tend to be more flexible by nature. Of the companies studied, 45 per cent of large enterprises were exploring Value 2.0 through flexibility, while only 2 per cent of start-ups were doing so.

Business leaders understand that this must change. All aspects of the enterprise should be designed not only to perform the task at hand in optimal fashion, but also to enable rapid change in order to drive superior performance.

Enterprises poised to capture Value 2.0 embrace this fundamental need for flexibility and are building this capability into all aspects of their enterprise. They are:

- Rethinking overall business design, taking a modular/component view of their enterprise which gives them a more structurally flexible model;
- Making hard decisions about which activities belong inside or outside the enterprise, based on a deeper understanding of which components deliver competitive advantage; and
- Adopting a service-oriented technology architecture that translates the business component model into IT services that support superior business performance today and greater IT flexibility tomorrow – and all at a lower cost.

These approaches to flexibility can reduce the internal cost of adjusting quickly to market forces and enable the enterprise to succeed in an era of accelerating change.

RULE #8: Foster rapid, collaborative innovation

In the Value 2.0 environment, new ways to collaborate and share knowledge, combined with greater transparency, are creating new forms of partnership while lowering the cost of innovating across enterprise silos.

Collaborative tools and social networking technologies are already providing higher levels of transparency and collaboration among organizations and their partners, customers and employees.

At the same time, cost hurdles for innovation have been lowered. Enterprises no longer require centralized research departments to be the sole contributors to the innovation pipeline. Social networking technologies and other collaborative tools enable more functions within the enterprise to drive innovation at a grassroots level.

Most importantly, enterprises are starting to recognize that speed is often more important than perfection when it comes to innovation. "Failing fast and failing cheap" or "launch and adapt" are strategies that echo the Web 2.0 paradigm of the "perpetual beta."[16] In this respect, large enterprises need to shift their thinking and to learn a great deal from multiple inexpensive, rapid failures, rather than learning a little from a single launch event.

Finally, new metrics must be developed to understand Value 2.0. Return on Investment (ROI) is useful to a certain degree, but it often does not capture the opportunity costs of missed innovation, network effects or value from communities. Restrictive metrics, along with restrictive control of ideation and incubation, can stifle innovation. Management systems need to adapt to create Value 2.0 through a "grassroots" collaborative innovation approach. This evolution is under way, but creating a new mindset takes time. Among the companies surveyed, only 5 per cent of large enterprises and 1 per cent of start-ups were focusing on Value 2.0 in this respect.

Putting the new rules into practice

The examples below show the effect that the new rules, used alone or in combination, can have on the performance of large enterprises. These organizations let networks do the work of creating, disseminating and amplifying knowledge. They reap benefits in terms of greater market share and customer intimacy. These Value 2.0-enabled enterprises are rapidly launching products and services that have been suggested, tested and co-created by communities. They are better able to change business models quickly and apply niche marketing tactics, for example, without alienating their core customer base. Their communities can guide them about which offerings to develop, which to maintain, and which to abandon gracefully.

Nintendo reclaims market share

Creating and capturing Value 2.0 is not an isolated event or a "quick win." Value 2.0 is created as a result of deliberate, thoughtful strategy about far-reaching business issues, taking into account new rules of value creation and the technologies that can enable them. Nintendo has recaptured market leadership in game consoles thanks to several factors: embracing customers more closely than competitors; reaching new customer segments with insights from these close relationships; and enabling a vibrant customer community.

After the early 1990s, when Nintendo held a strong leadership position and a market share of 68 per cent, competition greatly intensified (see Figure 4). By the mid-2000s its worldwide share of video game consoles had dropped from 61 per cent during the days of 16-bit game consoles, to just 22 per cent as the new 128-bit game systems were taking hold.[17] The 128-bit game consoles launched by Nintendo's competitors appealed to traditional hard-core gamers (18- to 26-year-old males) due to their technical superiority.

Figure 4. **Nintendo regains market share.**

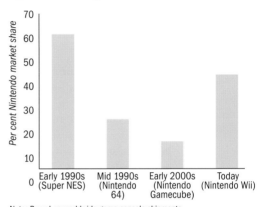

Note: Based on worldwide game console shipments.
Source: VGChartz.com, "Worldwide Hardware Shipments", October 2007, and Nintendo Co., Ltd.

The company's challenge was to attract new customers without alienating hard-core gamers. So Nintendo launched a community platform on the Web, offering incentives in exchange for product registration, feedback and profile information. Information captured this way provided critical customer insights and led to a loyalty program with a status aspect to it. "Sages" are an elite group of experienced gamers, handpicked by Nintendo staff based on the value and frequency of their community posting. In return for leading forums and helping new users, the "sages" gain access to exclusive game previews and other one-of-a-kind benefits.

By embracing customers through a web-based community with crowdsourced "sage" support, Nintendo was able to reconnect with older, casual male gamers, as well as women – two atypical segments for console game devices. In addition, Nintendo provided users with intuitive game controls in the Wii system, as well as an online library full of "nostalgic" game content – especially appealing to non-traditional customer segments.

Today, with 42 per cent market share, Nintendo has recaptured the lead over its competitors for the latest generation of game consoles.[18] By embracing customers and bringing brand advocates inside enterprise boundaries to provide key customer support and product feedback, Nintendo created and captured Value 2.0.[19]

IBM changes its culture

In 2001, IBM faced serious hurdles in engaging more than 300,000 employees worldwide to drive the kind of change needed to maintain market leadership. To meet the challenge, it created "WorldJam," the first in a series of massive, online discussions. These events used the Internet to support conversations among tens of thousands, hundreds of thousands and even millions of people. Initially "WorldJam" was an experiment to prove the power and ability of IBM's intranet to connect

Figure 5. IBM Jams: Collaborative innovation evolution, 2001 to 2006.

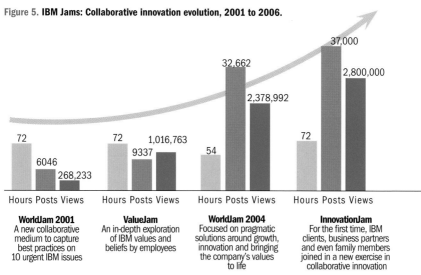

Source: IBM Jam Program Office.

and tap into its workforce. As a result of its success (more than 50,000 employees participated), IBM realized there were broader applications.

Subsequent jams have tackled big issues: company values; pragmatic solutions for growth; and, most recently, new market opportunities based on IBM's R&D capabilities. Jams have become part of IBM's

---

QUESTIONS TO CONSIDER

Capitalizing on new markets and business models

- What are the underserved segments in your marketplace? What have been the traditional barriers to serving them – cost, impact on existing customer segments or channel partners?
- Where is the "tipping point" of social software and emerging technology adoption among your customer segments? What does that tell you about your marketing strategy?
- How can you harness the liquidity and ubiquity of digital content in your marketplace? What customer and partner segments are your earliest indicators of this impact?
- What are the most information-intensive elements in your value chain? How is digitization affecting those elements? Can your business model handle those changes?
- With virtual worlds, how can 3D visualization and multi-user socialization enhance your products, services, brand image or even internal capabilities (training/learning)?
- How can a virtual experience become a brand enhancer for your enterprise?

Getting closer to your markets and customers

- What organizational barriers stop you inviting your customers inside the organization?
- What is your enterprise's ability to gather and extract value from the unstructured social interaction between you, your customers and your partners, or between your customer segments?
- How do you build and offer a rich experience or community based around your products and services? How can you stand out from the clutter of "me too" communities and offer customers something of value?

Creating new capabilities

- What is your company's "permission to innovate?" Are your non-R&D employees given explicit time or permission to focus on innovation and ideation? How do your management systems encourage innovative contributions beyond normal productive work?
- How socially connected are your employees? Compare that with the geographic distribution and isolation of your remote workforce.
- What social connections do you encourage beyond purely professional interaction?
- What passions, interests and expertise of your employees go unharnessed? What if they could pour those passions and energies into communities focused on product development, sales/marketing, service delivery or innovation?

---

management system, used as a collaborative management tool with a distinct business purpose, clearly understood objectives and desired outcomes. As shown in Figure 5, participation in these events increased six-fold between 2001 and 2006.

News of these events resulted in requests for IBM to help other organizations set up their own jams. These requests have come from the World Urban Forum for the United Nations' Habitat for Humanity and the Canadian government, and from an industry association – the Original Equipment Suppliers Association, based in the US. Often the impetus for these jams includes the need to drive change in culture, values or strategy. For example, global telecommunications equipment provider Nokia Siemens Networks held a jam to create new values after the merger of two large and culturally different companies. In addition, global consumer electronics manufacturer Nokia developed ideas to realize the company's new strategy, using the values created by the jam as a framework.

Initially a tool for social dialogue focused on cultural change, jams have expanded to become an enabler of Value 2.0 by harnessing the power of grassroots, collaborative innovation. They serve as just one example of many in which Value 2.0 is created and multiplied as disjointed, dispersed employees are connected to share knowledge, collaborate and drive innovation.

Conclusion: A critical proficiency for large enterprises

Value 2.0, when harnessed effectively, can be a significant source of advantage for large enterprises. Indeed, we anticipate that a Value 2.0 approach will evolve from being a "nice to have" initiative to being a critical capability for global corporations. The confluence of three factors – changing consumer preferences driven by the millennial generation; intensified globalization of competition; and the proliferation of fast-evolving social technologies that connect people and ideas – is what we believe will make Value 2.0 proficiency critical for global corporations in all industries. Value 2.0 will take hold at different paces in different industries, but make no mistake about it – employees, customers, partners and competitors are all changing how they interact with each other. For large companies, innovative, emerging technologies are becoming the key enablers for dealing with these disruptions and remaining competitive.

About the authors

Matt Porta is the Global Leader of IBM's Technology Strategy Consulting Practice and Service-Oriented Architecture Transformation within Global Business Services. He can be reached at matt.porta@us.ibm.com

Brian House is a Senior Consultant in IBM's Strategy and Change Practice in Global Business Services. His focus is on business model innovation, growth and marketing strategy, and the strategic implications of innovative technologies. He can be reached at bhouse@us.ibm.com

Lisa Buckley is a Managing Consultant in IBM's Global Business Services, where she focuses on IBM Jams: Collaborative Innovation, as well as innovative technologies and community-building. She can be contacted at lbuckley@us.ibm.com.

Amy Blitz is the Strategy and Change Lead for IBM's Institute for Business Value within Global Business Services. She can be reached at ablitz@us.ibm.com

Contributors

In the spirit of collaborative innovation, many colleagues throughout IBM and beyond – venture capitalists, analysts, and others – contributed to this paper. In particular, this paper would not have been possible without the substantial research contributions of Anubha Jain, Bindu Oleti, and Prasanna Pownsubbiah. The authors would also like to thank Wataru Sasamoto and his team for their contributions in identifying innovative start-ups. Thanks as well to Ray Bedard, Saul Berman, Marc Chapman, Eiji Hayashiguchi, Elissa Houchin, Deborah Kasdan, Aaron Kim, Bernie Michalik, and George Pohle (all of IBM) and Mark Raskino of Gartner and Oliver Young of Forrester for their insights and suggestions along the way.

References

1   IBM Corporation. "Expanding the Innovation Horizon: The Global CEO Study 2006." IBM Business Consulting Services. March 2006. http://www.ibm.com/bcs/ceostudy.

2   Wikipedia. Entry for "Craigslist." http://en.wikipedia.org/wiki/Craigslist. Based on alexa.com internet traffic data from December 29, 2006. Accessed on October 29, 2007.

3   Anderson, Chris. "The Long Tail." http://www.amazon.com/exec/obidos/ASIN/1401302378/bookstorenow600-20.

4   http://threadless.com. Accessed on July 25, 2007. http://www.saltworks.us. Accessed on October 18, 2007.

5   http://longtail.typepad.com/the_long_tail/2004/10/objection_1.html

6   "Prince Album Set Free on the Internet." BBC News. July 16, 2007. http://news.bbc.co.uk/2/hi/entertainment/6900792.stm.

7   Maki. "Radiohead's In Rainbows: A Look at Anti-Marketing in the Music Industry." Dosh Dosh. http://www.doshdosh.com/radiohead-anti-marketing-in-the-music-industry/.

8   Berman, Saul, Steven Abraham, Bill Battino and Louisa Shipnuck. "Navigating the Media Divide: Innovating and Enabling New Business Models." IBM Institute for Business Value. February 2007.

9   Virtual Worlds Management. "$1 Billion Invested in 35 Virtual Worlds Companies From October 2006 to October 2007." Virtual Worlds Management. October 2007. http://www.virtualworldsmanagement.com/2007/index.html.

10 Wu, Susan. "Virtual Goods: The Next Big Business Model." Techcrunch.com. June 20, 2007. http://www.techcrunch.com/2007/06/20/virtual-goods-the-next-big-business-model/.

11 Wladawsky-Berger, Irving. "Killer Apps and Virtual Worlds." Always On. August 7, 2007. http://alwayson.goingon.com/permalink/post/16876

12 Wikipedia. Entry for "Telepresence." http://en.wikipedia.org/wiki/Telepresence. Accessed on October 29, 2007.

13 "Focus on your meeting, not on your technology." Cisco: Telepresence. http://www.cisco.com/en/US/netsol/ns669/networking_solutions_solution_segment_home.html.

14 Hall, Kenji. "Nintendo Gives Design Power to the Player." *BusinessWeek*. September 27, 2006. http://www.businessweek.com/globalbiz/content/sep2006/gb20060927_472864.htm?chan=tc&chan=technology_technology+index+page_more+of+today's+top+stories.

15 Borland, John. "iTunes outsells traditional music stores." CNET News. November 21, 2005. http://www.news.com/iTunes-outsells-traditional-music-stores/2100-1027_3-5965314.html.

16 O'Reilly, Tim. "What is Web 2.0: Design Patterns and Business Models for the Next Generation of Software." O'Reilly. http://www.oreilly.com/pub/a/oreilly/tim/news/2005/09/30/what-is-web-20.html?page=4

17 VGChartz.com. "Worldwide Hardware Shipments." Accessed on October 30, 2007.

18 VGChartz.com. "Hardware Comparison Charts." Accessed on August 27, 2007;

19 Reuters. "Nintendo market value surpasses £42 billion." October 16, 2007. http://news.cnet.co.uk/gamesgear/0,39029682,49293415,00.htm; Nintendo Co. Ltd. Annual Report 2006. March 31, 2006. http://www.nintendo.com/corp/report/06AnnualReport.pdf.

"The nature of innovation — the inherent definition of innovation — has changed today from what it was in the past. It's no longer individuals toiling in a laboratory, coming up with some great invention. It's not an individual. It's individuals. It's multidisciplinary. It's global. It's collaborative."

Sam Palmisano, Chairman, President and CEO, IBM

"Innovation is viewed as a multi-dimensional concept, which goes beyond technological innovation to encompass ... new means of distribution, marketing or design. Innovation is ... an omnipresent driver for growth."

Erkki Liikanen, EU Commissioner for Enterprise and Information Society

Continuing to rethink innovation

A new Global CEO Study

While the studies presented here have helped answer many of the questions we had about innovation going into the CEO Study and the follow-on papers presented in this volume, they have also raised many new issues. In particular, our findings about the growing importance of business model innovation indicate that the nature of the enterprise itself is changing, perhaps dramatically. And so, as part of our continuing efforts to rethink innovation and a wide array of related issues, and, moreover, as the competitive landscape continues to change, we are launching a new Global CEO Study and a series of follow-on research efforts focused on various aspects of the enterprise of the future. We look forward to resuming this conversation with you, our reader, and with our extended global network of public and private sector leaders.

Marc Chapman, Saul Berman and Amy Blitz

FAST TH!NKING

Fast Thinking is a new concept in global publishing – a journal and web portal that draws together reports on innovative activity from all walks of life, from every field of endeavour, reflecting the impact of innovation and ultimately helping to drive innovation in the 21st century.

Fast Thinking is something different, more than a business journal and not your normal lifestyle magazine. A practical and thought-provoking read for those who are at the forefront of new thinking.

Fast Thinking is designed to be both practical and stimulating, inspired and inspiring, offering real-world services to an audience at a key point in their personal and professional lives.

Fast Thinking is as innovative in its own right as its audience. Every issue has editorial content that readers anticipate, share, discuss and keep for archiving and future reference.

Fast Thinking – the magazine for every thinking person. Subscribe online at www.FastThinking.com.au or secure your copy through Barnes & Noble.